THE ULTIMATE
PARENT TEACHER
INTERVIEW

THE ULTIMATE PARENT TEACHER INTERVIEW

A Guide For
Australian Parents

CHERYL LACEY

Copyright © 2017 by Cheryl Lacey

All rights reserved. No part of this book may be reproduced, stored in a retrieval system, or transmitted in any form or by any means, electronic, mechanical, photocopying, recording, or otherwise, without written permission from the publisher.

ISBN: 978-0-6482063-4-7 (paperback)

First Edition

DEDICATION

For my brother Craig

You are the light and the hope
for the most fulfilling journey of all –
parenthood.

The dragonfly symbolizes change, maturity,
and a greater understanding
of the deeper meaning of life.

ACKNOWLEDGEMENTS

As we travel our life path, we cross the paths of others. It's at these counterpoints where we experience our true purpose – to learn and to teach. I am blessed to have met so many extraordinary people at my counterpoints.

I extend my sincere gratitude to those who have taught me – especially my students and colleagues. Particular thanks go to Peter Hollingworth AC OBE, Susan Ryan, Sue Dyos, Heather Barton, Patricia Williams Hawke and Lyn Williams.

My very special thanks to my editor Janette Parr – there wouldn't be a book without your extraordinary talents.

To Kaye and Peter McCall OAM, for sharing the secrets of the ages – dignity, integrity, compassion and kindness.

To my two extraordinary daughters for making me a mum.

To Mum and Dad for the greatest of all gifts – our family.

To Clifton, for dancing with me.

To Taylor, Demi and Jesse – dream, believe, forgive.

To John – God Bless.

TABLE OF CONTENTS

Foreword xv

Introduction 3

How To Use This Book 13

1. From Home to School and Back 17
   - From home to school
   - From school to home
   - The parent-teacher meeting
   - Knowing your child
   - Summary
   - Taking the Lead

2. Schools and Life-Long Education 31
   - The first schools
   - Types of schools
   - Home – school – community – education
   - Summary
   - Taking the Lead

3. The Curriculum and What Lies Beneath 45
   - School and curriculum
   - The intended curriculum
   - Curriculum and pedagogy
   - Pedagogy in practice
   - Beyond the intended curriculum
   - Balancing the curricular and the extra curricular
   - Summary
   - Taking the Lead

4. The Professionals Who Teach Your Child. 61
   - To be a teacher
   - The makings of the teaching profession

- Teach for Australia
- Pedagogy – the art and science of teaching
- Roles and responsibilities
- Summary
- Taking the Lead

5. Becoming Literate - The Home School Connection. 75
    - Becoming literate
    - Lessons from the thrift store
    - Laying the foundations
    - The value of play
    - Home reading
    - Literacy, technology and the 21st century
    - Summary
    - Taking the Lead

6. Assessment and Reporting 93
    - What is assessment?
    - Types of assessments
    - Assessment and teacher judgement
    - Teacher judgement and your child
    - Reporting educational outcomes
    - Reporting to families
    - School performance and culture
    - Summary
    - Taking the Lead

7. Work-School-Family-Life Impact 113
    - Balancing school with life
    - The eight hour day
    - Homework
    - Disclosure
    - Finance, demographics and privacy
    - Summary
    - Taking the Lead

8. Taking the Lead. 131
- The family in the life of a child
- Advice to parents
- Schools and service to the community
- Balance and reason

CHECKLIST: Taking the Lead 141

A Final Note 147

Index 149

FOREWORD

By The Right Reverend and Honourable Peter Hollingworth ACE, OBE

When Cheryl Lacey describes this book as the 'The Ultimate Parent Teacher Interview – A Guide for Australian Parents,' she is referring to the range and extent of all those critical issues that will arise over the course of 13 years of education and learning at any child's school.

It has been written by someone who has had long-term, first-hand experience in being both a parent and a teacher. In Cheryl's case, her illustrations are meaningful and powerful experiences in her own life and career, which explains why her words have a ring of authority and authenticity.

Cheryl writes primarily in this instance as an advocate for parents and as an agent of change in seeking to improve the quality of the education in all our schools, with special reference to that critical relationship between the school, the home and the community. Yet as an experienced teacher, she comes to the task with a deep understanding of the difficulties that teachers confront in seeking to fulfil their professional obligations as education service providers on a daily basis.

This will be a valuable resource and guide, especially for those parents who are interested in gaining an historical understanding, as well as the basic grasp of the contemporary goals of their children's education. There is a considerable amount of detailed information offering many ways of how they themselves can be more effectively engaged as partners and active participants in their children's education at home and in their school communities.

For me, the book is a salutary reminder that education is a lifelong learning experience for all of us, even grandparents, and for all who have witnessed, and sometimes questioned, the rapid changes that have taken place in our lifetime.

Finally, I might say that I first met Cheryl in 2004 when we were both inducted as members of the Rotary Club of Melbourne. In being honoured to write this foreword, I am once again reminded of the gifts and skills expressed by the many Rotary colleagues whom I have met over the years.

Introduction

INTRODUCTION

As parents, we view schools as places of learning and teaching. And so they are. Because of that, it's easy to be swept up in conversations about the need for more school funding, less national testing, and better facilities to improve school performance. It's also understandable that we sympathise with teachers, and support their concerns about overwork, underpay, and disrespect.

But by staying on this narrow path, we might fail to realise that a school is capable of so much more.

A school is more than a space for learning and teaching. A school is a guardian of relationships. The most important is the one between you and your child, a relationship the school must acknowledge and protect. Most schools proudly claim a central role in the home-school-community interactions, but say little, if anything, about a genuine parent-teacher relationship, and how it can support parents and their children.

If genuine relationships are to move beyond policy and into reality, it is critical that you know and understand the strengths and limitations of your child's school and its staff. To nurture a school's strengths is to make a powerful contribution. To accept or expect teachers to deliver beyond their personal capabilities and professional accountabilities can be detrimental. Similarly, you must reject the school's expectations of you, which go beyond your own capacity. Establishing where to draw the lines might require you to take the lead. And the most respectful place to do it is in the parent-teacher interview.

I wrote this book to help you initiate these challenging but necessary conversations. Like you, I am a parent, but I am also a teacher. I want you to know that by taking the lead, through honest communication, your personal influence can be instrumental in helping your school to flourish, and your child to thrive.

Let me tell you how I arrived at writing this book.

Cast your mind back to 2001, to one of the most heartbreaking events of recent times – the attacks of September 11. Where were you when you heard the news? How did it affect you?

I was in New York that day. The impact on me was very real.

11 September 2001

Just four days earlier, my five-year-old daughter and I had moved from Melbourne to New York.

INTRODUCTION

I was living my dream – doing the two things I loved best: being a mum and inspiring school leaders to raise the bar of the teaching profession.

On the morning of September 11, I had commenced work – consulting with teachers in a large Brooklyn public school. As I walked past the office, I heard an administrator yell: "Oh my God, a plane has hit the Pentagon".

Within minutes I was thrust into taking a lead, with the principal, operating with calm and order, but with no details other than the school was in lockdown.

I thought immediately of my own daughter, in school, several suburbs away. I had no way of reaching her. Was a leader watching over her, just as I was helping to care for 900 children and dozens of staff? Did she know that I was desperate to be with her? Was she as scared as I was?

The day was a surreal blur. As the morning's events continued to unfold, we responded to departmental instructions, consoled staff who had family and friends working in downtown Manhattan, and co-ordinated security pick-ups for panicked parents desperate to have their children close. Amidst all the activity, we maintained a positive and professional front – encouraging teachers to continue as best they could, and distracting the children until we knew more.

I finally reached my daughter at 5pm. She was the last remaining child at the school. Both shocked and elated to see me, she said, "I thought you were gone and I would have to find a new mummy". It rocked my identity to the core.

What had I done that day? Why hadn't I run to my daughter?

Was I wrong to feel angry that in helping reconnect mothers with their children, I was disconnected from mine? Was I wrong to care that the principal valued my ability to help lead in such a difficult situation? Was I wrong to stay put, and remain the consummate professional? Wasn't I a mother? Wasn't I a teacher? Could I be both? What was I?

No-one wanted to stay at school that day – but some had to. Everyone wanted to be with loved ones – but some couldn't.

That tragic day wasn't a working day for me; it was a day of profound despair. It was the day when my two selves – mother and teacher – collided. Fear gave way to focus. Reasoning tempered my desire to flee. Adrenalin and a deep knowing fuelled my actions.

13 September 2001

Two days later, the harsh reality of my new life had begun. I returned to working in schools with metal detectors, wire fences, and barred windows. We were living with high alert security, while at the same time maintaining the heartbeat of the community – its school. I attended funerals for the victims, and scanned 'missing person' posters, but also skipped down the street with my daughter, as though the world were one big rainbow.

The events of those days represented a turning point for me. In schools, I was embraced as a professional, yet denied ready access as a parent. As a consultant at my daughter's school, the security staff would greet me with a smile as I arrived each day. I would happily hand over my identification, and be signed in, before walking up the steps to the office and beyond. By contrast, when I attended in my capacity as parent, there'd be no smile or greeting, but a series of questions, and a demand for evidence of my right to be there. My curiosity turned to sadness. Parents rarely entered school buildings and usually remained outside the school gate. It became increasingly clear that my profession gave me privileges they were denied. The great divide between home and school, and the sheer hypocrisy of all that schools claimed to stand for, were clear.

Witnessing New York's psychological recovery from the 9/11 attacks, and working in a school system that was new to me, helped me identify the path I wanted to take. Since becoming a teacher, more than a decade before, I had wanted passionately to nurture the genuine parent-teacher relationship, but I knew that, first, I had a lot of learning and healing to do.

Now, more than a decade later, I realise that September 11 was the beginning of my agitation for effecting change on a global level, and my motivation was intensified by what I call 'mother guilt'. How could I accept that to be the best parent for my child, I might sometimes have to be a better professional to achieve it?

Today, I can finally accept that on that fateful day I did not fail my daughter. I also know that my daughter's teacher did not fail me. We both did what we could for *mother and child*. We honoured our professional accountability to protect and assist the children in our charge. And the line was drawn there. We did not become *mother for child*.

As you read this book, you'll be immersed in a collection of stories that have influenced my view of genuine parent-teacher relationships. There are also some suggestions on building on what you already have to create a mutually respectful and genuine parent-teacher relationship. You already have your child's best interest at heart.

Don't ever apologise for demanding the best for your child. Don't be afraid to ask questions. Always make sure you feel totally comfortable with anyone who influences your child's life.

This is what I hope that you will take away from this book:

1. **Enthusiasm** – for honest communication in your school community.
2. **Confidence** – expect teachers to deliver to their best abilities.
3. **Compassion** – support teachers to relinquish what is beyond their capability.
4. **Inspiration** – think big, think beyond, and lead the way toward genuine parent-teacher relationships.

Most importantly, I know you will trust your instincts, as you take the lead for your child.

Shall we begin?

How To Use This Book

HOW TO USE THIS BOOK

All parents have this experience in common. It's what I call 'the sandpit moment'. You'll recognise it. Your child is playing alongside another. Someone throws sand, and both children begin to cry. Your immediate reaction is to protect your child. The other child's mother reacts in the same way. Usually, there is a congenial outcome and both children learn some valuable lessons – about personal space, resilience, or getting along with others.

But it doesn't always work that way.

You might have stories about those times, as well – about different points of view expressed, different values defended and, dare I say it, allegations made. In cases like this, how do you react? You want to protect your child, but at the same time you don't want to appear too assertive. Either way, you have a choice. Being the voice for your child is not about being right or wrong; it's about contributing to a resolution when facts and opinions are out of balance.

Today you could say we have windows into one another's lives, hearts and minds. The world is on our doorstep and always at our fingertips. The sandpit is

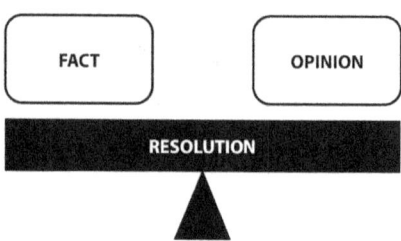

global as well as local. But while your children are growing up, the sandpit is often the school and the classroom.

This book is about these moments and the impact they have on us, on our children and on their education. Like you, I have hundreds of stories – sandpit moments from my role as a teacher, as a parent, and as both.

In each chapter I share some of these stories, as well as information about education, schools and the parent-teacher relationship. At the end of each chapter, you'll find a summary of the main points, and a list of actions you might take if you want to advocate for a genuine parent-teacher relationship, via an informative parent-teacher interview.

Finally, I've made a checklist that will help you to become an advocate for your child, and an active participant in times of imbalance.

From Home to School and Back

Chapter 1
FROM HOME TO SCHOOL AND BACK

T.E.A.C.H. = **T**o **E**ducate **A** **C**hild **H**o*nourably*

The morning my eldest daughter started school, I did two things. I greeted her teacher with warmth and respect. Then I burst into tears.

The scene was familiar. I'd been in many like it, since I was in my 20s. But this time my role was different. Then, I was the teacher, and childless. Now, I was the parent, and handing over my 5-year-old daughter, whom I had adopted from Thailand just 18 months earlier. It was awfully distressing. First, because my daughter was reluctant to let go of me. Second, because I knew I could no longer protect her. Third, because the concept of parents putting blind faith in teachers, which I had previously experienced as a professional, was now a personal and grave reality for me as a mother.

From home to school

From the moment we become parents, the full responsibility of raising our children rests squarely on our shoulders. Parenting is no easy task; neither is the task of navigating the many services that help us raise our children. Whatever your personal circumstances, though, you have a voice. You can choose your general practitioner, your private health care provider, your specialist, and infant health service. You decide on your playgroup, your babysitter, and childcare centre. Navigating and selecting services becomes a major part of your responsibility as a parent. You are the decision maker.

But then, one day, our children commence compulsory schooling. We hand them over to individuals we know very little about. And the older our children get, the less we are likely to know about the various teachers they have.

But it hasn't always been this way.

Long before schools were established, wealthy parents sought tutors to build knowledge, positive judgement and wisdom in their children. Confucius (551 BC – 479 BC), regarded as the world's first private tutor, was a master at this, and developed trusting relationships – first with parents and then with his students. An invitation to tutor a child was an invitation to nurture ethical citizenship in the next generation. It was considered a great honour.

For centuries, parents have carefully chosen highly regarded individuals – including people of faith, philosophers, and the well-educated – to contribute to the education of their children. Today, although some parents still invest in subject-specific tutors, compulsory schooling has replaced the parent as the direct employer, and the teacher has replaced the carefully chosen tutor.

From school to home

In my workshops I'm constantly asked: What's the best approach to stop parents questioning the learning and teaching taking place in schools? It's the wrong question. Parents have every right to know and understand *exactly* what is happening in schools. Much better questions are: What changes are needed to make sure parents are better informed? How can we ensure genuine parent-teacher relationships? And more importantly: What do parents need to know in order to 'take the lead' in their child's education?

Let's start with relationships.

Figure 1 shows how schools currently view themselves. You'll see that your child is placed at the centre of the home, school, and community relationship. This is common in all schools and is the viewpoint from which school systems make decisions. This is

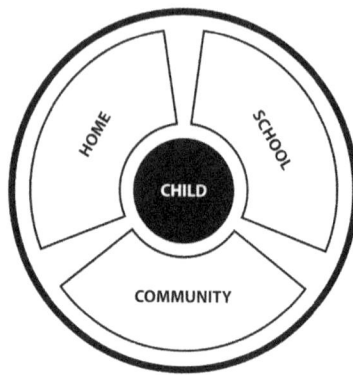

Figure 1: Misrepresentation of Schools Value

a cause for concern. The problem is that the school sees itself as a partner of equal influence, rather than as a service provider. Schools don't raise children – parents do! Schools provide the service of teaching that assists you in the education of your children.

If you were placed at the centre, with your child, then schools would be in a healthier position to create that genuine parent-teacher relationship and targeted service. Figure 2 shows how this might look.

Your immediate point of contact with your child's school is with the teacher. And because the Principal and the School Board determine the teacher's accountabilities to your child, it makes sense that they too must be central to your relationship with the school.

If you are to take the lead in your child's education, it is essential you know what is expected of your

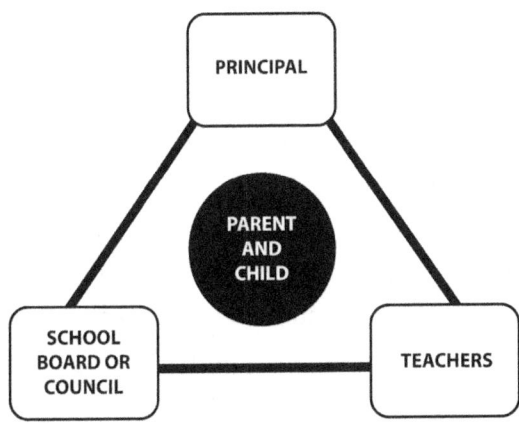

Figure 2: Parent as Leader in Child's Education

child's teachers, the strengths they bring to their roles, and the support available to them to provide the service for which they are qualified. The most appropriate place for you to find out these things is in a parent-teacher interview.

The parent-teacher meeting

Every school organises a parent-teacher meeting or conference. It is the primary arrangement for managing the relationship between parent and teacher, and is more or less guarded by school policy and time constraints. The purpose of these meetings is to discuss your child's progress in school. They are offered in primary and secondary schools, and usually scheduled at the beginning and in the middle of the school year.

In special circumstances, teachers might schedule a meeting at other times during the year, and there are generally processes in place for you to request a meeting too, when necessary.

When you consider the finer details of these meetings, however, you might reach the same conclusion as I have; these meetings are flawed, and limit the potential of a genuine parent–teacher relationship. I say this for several reasons.

First, primary school teachers spend an average of 4.5 hours per day with your child. In a full school year – 40 weeks of class time – that's approximately 900 hours. A parent-teacher meeting is limited to 10 minutes, and even as few as 5 minutes in some secondary schools. With such time constraints, how does a teacher decide what to share and what to leave out? How much time is available for a Q and A or, more importantly, for joint decision-making about your child's learning?

Second, these interviews take place at a time and place determined by the school. A 10-minute interview at the convenience of school staff might have negative implications for parents. Travel time, loss of wages, changes in family arrangements, and the costs of fuel, transport or childcare aren't usually considered. A 10-minute interview can add up to several hours for many parents. How do costs and lost time stack up at your end?

Third, the meeting is intended to provide feedback about your child's learning. The focus is on learning that occurs as a result of teaching. Unless you have a teaching degree, it isn't easy to understand all the elements that go together to create cohesive conditions for effective learning. Creating those conditions is the teacher's job. The meeting should focus sharply on your understanding of how they contribute to your child's education.

You'll notice I mentioned 40 weeks of class time. That leaves 8 weeks, or 304 hours, of pupil-free time for teachers. What if a 10-minute meeting were converted to a 1- or 2-hour parent-teacher interview? Imagine how much more real information you would gain about your child, and your child's teacher (see Figure 3).

In my opinion, that's certainly worth thinking about!

Knowing your child

When my eldest daughter was in first grade, her classroom teacher was also the maths coordinator for the school. Unfortunately, this meant that she spent a lot of time working with other teachers to improve their teaching of maths, while a substitute taught maths to my daughter's class.

By the time my daughter reached Year 3 she had lost her confidence in maths and would become

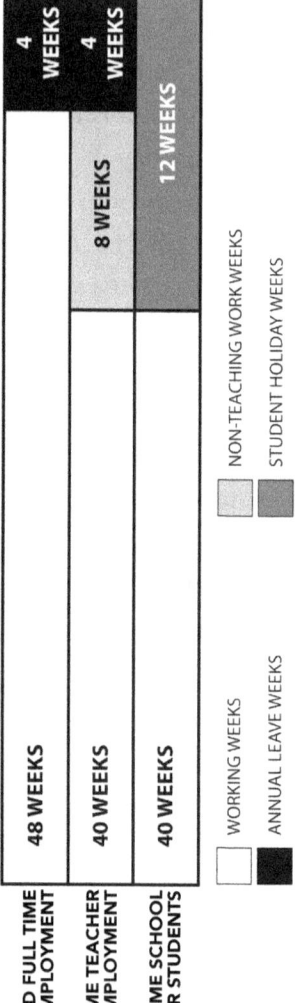

Figure 3: Non-Teaching Time for Possible Parent - Teacher Interview

stressed if she had any homework related to maths. I raised my concerns at the mid-year parent-teacher meeting, and was told that she was doing just fine, and that there was nothing to worry about.

While this didn't sit comfortably with me, I accepted her teacher's word and shared his positive thoughts with my daughter. She didn't mention maths again and school life went by without any further concern regarding her maths.

Several years later, when my daughter was in Middle School, her anxiety levels rose again with regard to maths homework. It was found that she was well behind the expected level and required intensive support to consolidate the basics – including times tables and multiplication. Her Middle School maths teacher was very strict, had very high expectations, and willingly accepted my requests to meet on a regular basis. She provided tremendous support and helped my daughter regain her confidence. Furthermore, she could not understand how my daughter had managed to bluff her way through primary school maths.

No doubt you have heard the phrase, '*Street angel – house devil*'. Keep this in mind with regard to school and home life. How children are viewed in school is not always how parents see them at home. More important, your child is one student at the school, and one of many in a class. Children learn ways to behave and manage differently in the many circumstances they find themselves, and with the different teachers from one subject to another, and from one year to the next.

My daughter managed to hide her anxiety about maths and, as a result, some of her needs weren't met. When it came up again later, her Middle School maths teacher was there to support her. It wasn't my job to 'back fill' when my daughter fell behind. It was my job to notify the school and ensure my daughter's learning was managed there – not at home.

Teachers provide a service to you; that service is teaching. Be sure to understand what that service is, and how it is delivered. Without sufficient awareness, it is difficult to take that central position in the school's relationship with your child. Don't be afraid to speak up and make a stand for your child.

Summary

So far we have covered the following points:

- You are responsible for raising your child. Schools provide one of the many services available to assist you with this life-long responsibility.
- Compulsory schooling has changed parents' involvement in their child's education.
- Teachers have a minimum of 8 working weeks when students are not present.
- The parent-teacher meeting is limited to 5 or 10 minutes, twice per year.

Taking the Lead

Use this discussion starter for taking the lead in your child's education:

- What steps do I need to take to replace the 10-minute parent-teacher meeting with a 1-hour parent-teacher interview?

Schools and Life-Long Education

Chapter 2
SCHOOLS AND LIFE-LONG EDUCATION

An authentic educator views learning through a compassionate lens.

Not long ago, I had the privilege of working as a volunteer with *Koala Kids*. It's an extraordinary organisation dedicated to children and young people undergoing cancer treatment, and its mission is to bring happiness to them and to their families. It does this by providing year-round activities at children's cancer wards in Victorian hospitals. With the support of my youngest daughter's gymnastics club, my first major volunteer experience was to help organise Olympics Day – particularly exciting because Olympian gymnast Georgia Bonora had agreed to participate.

It's not every day you get to rub shoulders with an Olympian, and for these children and their families, the opportunity came as a complete surprise. There was equipment set up for physical involvement on the day, but more important was the stimulus for connection and communication.

As the day unfolded, it was fascinating to watch the children. Some actively participated with Georgia, while others sat to one side and crept slowly toward passive involvement. There was such wonderful interaction between gymnast and child – a knowing, and a level of trust and anticipation. The hospital staff watched proudly as the children they'd come to know so well became immersed in a happy distraction from the implications of their medical challenges. Parents encouraged and nurtured the children, and beamed with pride. They were nurtured, too, by the genuine connections felt by everyone in the room. But it wasn't until all the children, some gravely ill, were invited to stand on the foam winners' box for Georgia to present them with a chocolate Gold Medal, that the picture was complete.

Georgia was more than an Olympic champion that day; she became a compassionate educator. She intuitively knew each child's capacity, with its measure of reluctance or confidence. She also had a great deal in common with them. They all understood resilience, the striving to win against all odds, and the need for the support and faith of others. She didn't assume the right to engage with the children without first creating a safe place for them, and then having the support and approval of their mums or dads.

The Olympics Day was a great illustration of the central role parents have in their child's education. Schools must see that role in the same way.

The first schools

It has been said that the very first public school began in 459 BC. It was the 'house of the book' or the 'house of the teacher', and it was established in Jerusalem by a Jewish scribe and priest, known as Ezra. The purpose of his school was to provide education for fatherless boys, aged sixteen and upward. The Jewish community continued to take the lead, and determined that all children, regardless of class, were entitled to an education. The result: the beginnings of what we now know as elementary or primary schools.

During the middle ages, monasteries and the Roman Catholic Church were centres of education. So were the town squares, where culture was passed on to groups of people who gathered there to read, or listen. Anyone could open a school and present a curriculum offering. In that way parents could choose the right school for their children, based on what they wanted them to learn and the fee that they could afford.

Centuries later, between the 1870s and 1950s, the segregation laws in the Southern United States extended to public schools. Government support for Black education was poor, so parents turned to churches, which became not only places of worship but also places of learning and teaching.

The First Fleet arrived in Australia in 1788. The law of the day had made no provision for education, so it was left to convict women and the wives of the marines, to tutor the children.

These are brief glimpses into some of the many historical accounts that place parents at the centre of the schooling and life-long education of their children. Selecting the right school for your child is the first step towards taking a central role. If your child is already in school, there is no harm in re-evaluating your choice.

Types of schools

Schools play a vital role in our lives. We all have recollections of the great, the good and the not-so-good experiences of our school years. And, while schools might be considered the bedrock of childhood and the heartbeat of a community, no two are the same. Every school, however, is part of a system or association that has agreed regulations, registration requirements and philosophical values. Figure 4 shows the types of schools currently available in Australia.

SCHOOLS AND LIFE-LONG EDUCATION

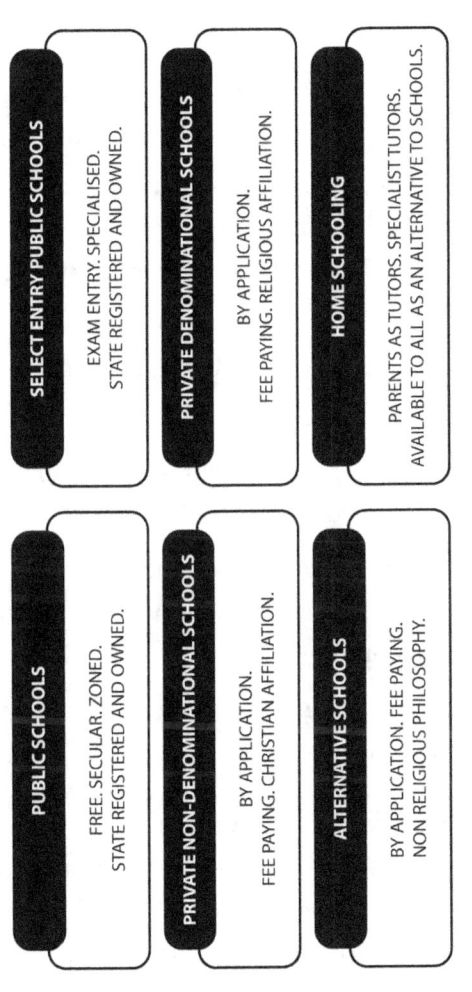

Figure 4: Types of Schools

Public schools

Most parents think of public schools as being free, compulsory and secular. However, in practice, they're not. By the 1870s, Australia had undergone a transition; the various (mostly penal) settlements had become six sovereign colonies, and Public Education Acts were established under the constitution of each. The purpose was to provide free, compulsory and secular education. It also meant:

- Colonies (later States) had control of their own public schools
- State financial aid to church based schools was abolished
- Local control, by families and the community, was removed, leaving the Minister with central control
- Christian values underpinned morality in public schools.

It could be said, however, that the States have never fully, and collectively, exercised the law of free, compulsory and secular education.

For the families of children who commence public school in 2014, and who study to Year 12, the estimated cost will be $63K, in metropolitan areas, and $51K in regional areas. This is a huge expense, and negates any suggestion that public education is free[1]. Truancy remains a major issue across the country. In 2014, for example, more than 9300 students in Western Australian public schools were deemed to be at 'severe risk' because they attended school less than 60% of the time.

To be classified as 'secular', a school should not have a connection with religious or spiritual matters. The singing of Christmas Carols, and a visit from the Easter Bunny for Foundation classes still have a place, however, in many public schools, as does a strong emphasis on indigenous studies – including spirituality.

So if the concept of free, compulsory and secular education doesn't really exist, then what do public schools offer? When I ask parents this question, the most common answers usually include ideas about 'local families', 'local kids' and the 'local school – the heartbeat of the community'. In practice, they are referring to zoning, where local families have priority when securing places for their children in the local public school.

Select entry public schools

As I noted earlier in this chapter, no two schools are the same; select entry public schools are a great example. These schools provide an enriched curriculum

---
1. Australian Scholarship Group, 2014 survey

for high-achieving students. To be accepted, and to retain a place, in one of these schools, students must sit a common entrance exam and yearly exams thereafter. Select entry public schools might have unique offerings, including gender specific enrolment, or curriculum specialisation – for example in languages, or science and technology.

Independent denominational and non-denominational schools

Many Australian schools, including those established prior to the introduction of the public school system, feature religious faith as a core value. Due to the introduction of secular public schools and State Public Education laws these schools do not receive State funding – leaving parents responsible for the payment of school fees. Despite the cost, parents select these schools as a complement to their own faith and values.

Independent philosophical schools

While most independent schools are affiliated with a religious tradition, such as Christianity, Judaism or Islam, some are connected neither to spiritual nor religious ideology, but are shaped instead by non-religious philosophical aims and values. Examples are the Montessori and Community schools. Although these schools must be registered, they have the capacity to differentiate the curriculum. They are also fee-paying schools.

Home schooling

School isn't for everyone. Some families choose to take on the responsibility of teaching their children at home. This doesn't necessarily mean home schooling is a casual arrangement; registration is required by the State in which the home schooled child resides. Among the benefits of home schooling is access to the approved national or State curriculum, as well as the freedom to choose specialist tutors, social activities, and community involvement.

Home – school – community – education

What's the difference between the best school in the worst street and the worst school in the best street? The answer is simple: its community. A community is a group that has particular attitudes and interests in common. A school is not only part of the wider community, it is a community within itself; this means education flows within and beyond the school boundaries. Each member of the community, however, must clearly understand the shared attitudes or values, and the interests of each child must be paramount. A genuine parent-teacher partnership can achieve all this, and starts with an understanding of what a school has to offer.

As a parent, you have every right to understand all that relates to schooling – particularly the faith and/or the educational philosophy the school follows and offers. Don't be afraid to ask questions. These are your children. You have every right to advocate for the education you want them to have. The key is knowing exactly what the school values, and precisely what it contributes.

Summary

In this chapter we have covered the following points:

- History teaches us a great deal about schools and education.
- The first public school was known as the 'house of the book'.
- The school is just one of the places where education occurs.
- Australian schools had an affiliation to faith.
- Public Schools in Australia are owned and controlled by each State.
- Parents have a choice of public, independent or home schools.
- Schools are communities where attitudes and interests are shared and held in common.

Taking the Lead

Use these action starters for taking the lead in your child's education:

- Make a bullet list of what you know about your school's values.

- Review the school's policies on faith, philosophy and curriculum.

- Compile a list of questions to ask your child's teacher.

The Curriculum and What Lies Beneath

Chapter 3
THE CURRICULUM AND WHAT LIES BENEATH

*Sometimes we get more than we need;
other times we need more than we get.*

The first pair of work shoes I ever purchased were gumboots. They kept my feet dry as I walked across the muddy fields of rural Victoria where my teaching career began. I was fortunate. Mine was one of those typical country classrooms, complete with blackboard and coat hooks; the original school bell hung outside its front door. And my role was to teach 18 foundation students – one of whom was disabled.

This was during the 80s – a time of great change in Victorian education. A major initiative had been the closure of special schools and, for children with disabilities, the introduction of open enrolment into local public schools. I was passionate about this initiative. Having done community work in a special school while in Year 10, and just enrolled in a Bachelor of Education with a major in special education – the area in which I had planned eventually to work – you can imagine how thrilled I was with my first appointment.

Max was such a loveable child. He was extremely popular with both students and teachers. The small close-knit community seemed to add something more to his enthusiastic presence. The students loved taking turns pushing Max's wheelchair, and the teachers enjoyed giving him a high-five or inviting him to join the lunchtime basketball games. His disabilities, however, were very complex, and his needs went far beyond requiring a wheelchair. The implications soon became clear. I was not a good fit for the position.

Like all primary teachers at that time, I had graduated with a Diploma of Primary Education. This study qualified me as a generalist classroom teacher. It did not provide me with any of the knowledge or expertise I required to cater for Max's very special needs. As a graduate, I had no experience in navigating policies, departmental procedures, union matters, support services or, more importantly, the expectations of success that came from such a close knit community. Most of all, I didn't know how to look after myself, or get the assistance I needed, to offer full support to Max and his parents.

I struggled for five months. I was teaching a mainstream class and, as in most classes, there were children of varying capabilities and needs. At the same time I tried to meet Max's personal curricular needs, but he needed more support than I could provide – more, as it turned out, than any of us could provide. The integration aides employed by the school also struggled with the complexities of what Max required, the details of which it would not be appropriate to share here.

The situation caused tremendous anguish for all of us. We really wanted Max to be with us, but he needed more specialised teaching. A mainstream classroom, and a generalist teacher like me, just weren't enough. Worse still, my other students were also suffering. The time I spent working with Max and supporting his aide, bled into the one-to-one time I needed to have with my other students. It was overwhelming.

I campaigned heavily for a more balanced curriculum – for Max, for my class, and for Max's parents. My final attempt was to seek support from the teacher's union – but none arrived. When Max's integration support person resigned, I was devastated. I had learned, however, one of the most powerful lessons about my profession: the curriculum and the introduction of departmental policy – in this case the integration of disabled children into mainstream schools – are not always achieved in reality. This was my sharp introduction to the elements that lie beneath the curriculum.

School and curriculum

The Latin word *curriculum* means a course that is run, which might best explain how it is related to schools and education. However, our understanding of curriculum, which means 'that which is learned', goes back to the beginning of time, when hunters and gatherers taught their loved ones to hunt, fish, gather food, find water, carve rocks, and live with others. Learning was essentially about life and survival. We could almost say that hunters and gatherers established the first known curriculum – a curriculum for living.

Schools on the other hand, began as organisational structures. They enabled groups of people to be taught at the same time. Originally established to provide moral and ethical principles for living, schools evolved as society developed.

With the division and ownership of land came the concept of social class, which created a further distinction between education and schooling. The ruling class enjoyed a sophisticated curriculum that included grammar, rhetoric and logic, while the working class received basic instruction in literacy and numeracy, and were taught life skills, such as agriculture, that were learned as they worked in the fields. In the wake of the Industrial Revolution, the use of children for labour meant schooling was little more than teaching the basic skills necessary for working in a factory or mine to earn a living.

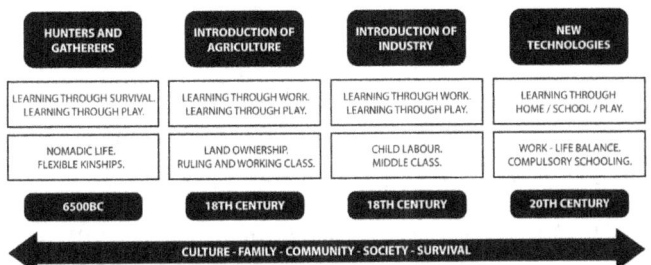

Figure 5: Work and School Life

Today the emphasis, in society and in schools, is on new technologies and the preparation of children for 21st century employment.

The intended curriculum

When a school is registered, it is approved to deliver what is called the intended curriculum. This includes broad, written statements that reflect what students should know, understand, and be able to do, by the end of each school year. The intended curriculum is developed at the national or state level and sets a framework of expectations or standards with regard to what all students should be taught – regardless of where they live or what their circumstances might be. It is intended to ensure a degree of consistency across all schools.

Curriculum, however, is also adapted at the school and classroom levels, to achieve a better match with student backgrounds, available resources, and other factors. In other words, although there is a broad intended curriculum, every school and classroom has its own variation. Added to this are the skills and knowledge a teacher requires in order to deliver the intended curriculum – skills that are not only incredibly complex, but unique to the individual. It's not hard to see, then, that the national or state curriculum schools are intended to provide might not necessarily correspond with what is delivered.

Curriculum and pedagogy

In professional circles, teaching is often better known as pedagogy. A simple definition of pedagogy is 'the art and science of teaching'. Pedagogy encompasses all that teachers are – all that they bring to their teaching and the unique way in which they deliver the intended curriculum. All teachers have their own unique pedagogy or 'professional DNA'. Figure 6 is a visual map that shows what I believe pedagogy to be. The message I am conveying here is that every teacher has an individual and unique responsibility for the delivery of the intended curriculum.

Pedagogy in practice

A number of years ago, as a Year 4 teacher, I set a publishing assignment for my students. I chose the genre – an alphabet book – and each student chose a topic. It was a creative way to meet some of the intended curriculum, including presentation skills, studying a genre, and building word study skills.

To conclude the assignment, we planned a book launch, where students would share their published works with parents and friends.

Some of the topics the children chose were an obvious match for their age and maturity – topics such as animals, colours, food and plants. Others were more specific, and included things like spices and breeds of dogs. One student chose STDs – sexually transmitted diseases.

I felt extremely uncomfortable with his choice – particularly given my students were only 9 and 10 years of age – so I invited the young boy to choose another, more appropriate, topic.

The next morning, I was called to a meeting with the boy's parents and the school principal. His parents held the view that their son was being discriminated against and denied the opportunity to express his creativity. My principal's response was, "Parents are always right. Allow the STD topic".

For me, the issue wasn't simply that of one boy's creativity. There were 31 other students and their parents to consider. So I suggested a compromise. I would agree to the STD topic on the condition that every parent from my class provided consent for their children to be present when this boy's book was

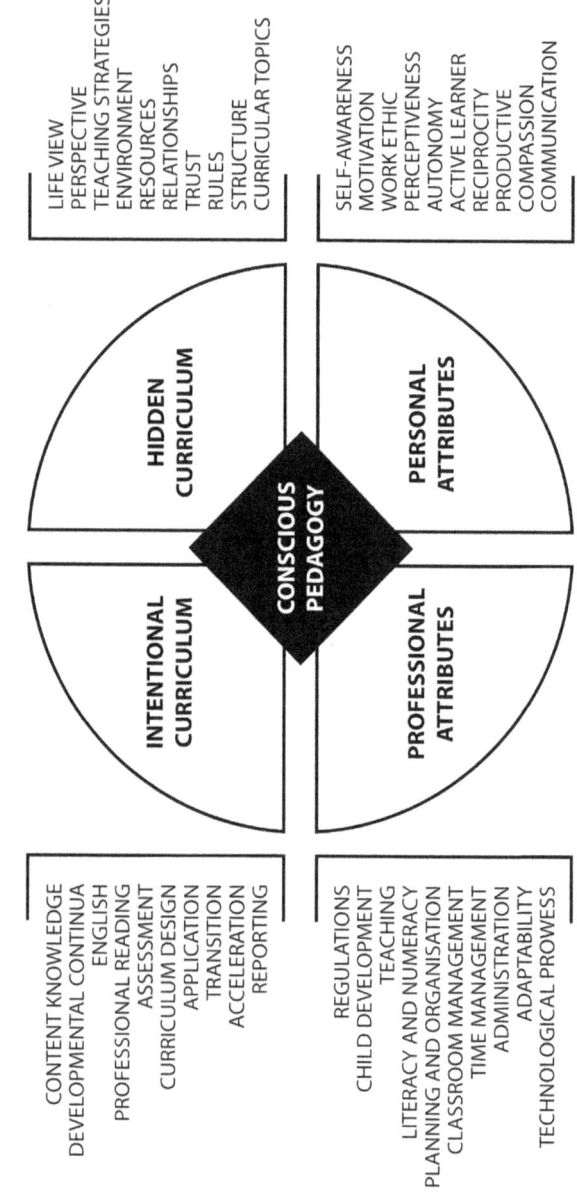

Figure 6: Pedagogy

launched. After further discussion, which included the parent's concerns about potential isolation and denial of equality, they realised I would not back away from protecting the rights of the remaining students. They agreed to the matter of consent. The outcome was that their son completed the assignment at home and read it to me in a one-to-one setting. No parents signed consent forms, and no other students were present.

Fast forward to two years later. I was teaching a foundation class in the same school. The intended curriculum included the topic of Change and Lifecycles. We began by studying caterpillars and butterflies. Such was the interest in the topic that it led to my students discussing the human lifecycle.

One morning I was confronted by a parent who informed me her son didn't have a penis; he had a 'willy'. She was appalled that the word 'penis' had been used in the classroom. Once again, I found myself in the principal's office. And once again, I found myself defending the parent group as a whole. I explained that students were naming body parts, and I felt obliged to correct any misused terms. The parent was not against my teaching the life cycle topic, and could appreciate what I had done; however, she still had reservations. It was a most productive meeting, which resulted in a whole class parent information evening, where we agreed upon the content and limitations of the lifecycle study. The meeting and the topic were a huge success, and resulted in a more thorough year-long focus on health and wellness.

Beyond the intended curriculum

The example above describes the impact of pedagogy on the intended curriculum. It particularly highlights, to some degree, the hidden curriculum outlined in Figure 6. The combination of these – intended curriculum + pedagogy + hidden curriculum – is what is referred to as the actual curriculum: in other words, what has in fact been *taught*.

We know that with teaching comes learning. The end result of the intended curriculum is what is known as the achieved curriculum – in other words, the extent to which students know, understand, or can do what was stated in the intended curriculum. (see Figure 7).

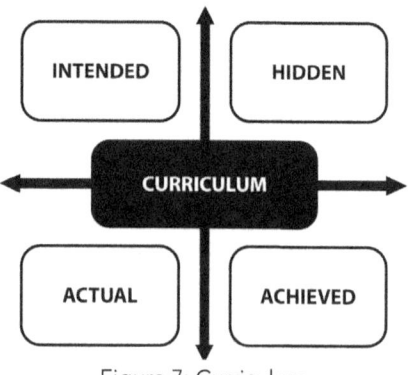

Figure 7: Curriculum

And that brings us back to the art and science of teaching. A teacher must work through an incredibly complex process – to understand what is intended, to match it with the students' current skill sets, and then to deliver what is expected. When a teacher brings all these elements together, and the learning and teaching outcomes are met, it is an extremely rewarding experience for all concerned.

Balancing the curricular and the extra curricular

Just as every school is unique, so too is the intended curriculum that is offered. In terms of depth, for example, not all schools have specialist art teachers, which might mean that some elements of the art curriculum are loosely embedded in other areas of the curriculum.

As we have seen, education takes place beyond the intended curriculum the school provides. One example of this is extra-curricular education – opportunities or experiences that fall outside the intended curriculum. It's common for parents to provide these for their children; your child might, for instance, learn to play a musical instrument with a private tutor.

The question you should ask is this: What impact does this have on the curriculum that is offered at the school? Take time to compare the extra-curricular experiences you provide with the intended curriculum your child's school provides. Be sure to discuss it with your child's class teacher. It might be possible for your child to be excused from participating in some of the intended curriculum, allowing sharper focus on other curriculum areas requiring attention.

Summary

Here's a snapshot of what we have covered in this chapter:

- **Pedagogy** is the art and science of teaching
- **Curriculum** is developed at national and state level
- Schools and teachers can adapt the national and State curriculum
- The **intended curriculum** is an overview of what is expected to be taught
- The **hidden curriculum** includes those characteristics of the school and the teacher that affect the delivery of the intended curriculum
- The **actual curriculum** is what has been delivered
- The **achieved curriculum** is what has been taught and learned
- Out of school opportunities can duplicate or reach beyond the intended curriculum

Taking the Lead

Use these action starters for taking the lead in your child's education:

- Review your child's school curriculum.
- Highlight any key phrases you do not understand.
- Seek clarification on what the intended curriculum is.
- Compile a list of questions to ask your child's teacher.

The Professionals
Who Teach Your Child

Chapter 4
THE PROFESSIONALS WHO TEACH YOUR CHILD

Change comes from embracing success and failure.

You might have heard the term 'backstory'. It refers to the history or background that actors create for the characters they portray in stage, film or television productions. In fact, this is what actors are paid for – the construction of the backstory, and then the acting out of that character's role, for our entertainment.

Using backstory is also a method for helping professionals identify what motivates them to work in a particular field of endeavour. The differences are that the backstories aren't constructed, and the characters are real. The aim of this method is to pinpoint an event, or a person's interpretation of an event, that led to that person's work choice. For example, my passion is teaching and learning, and I feel it so deeply that I know I chose it as a vocation, or calling; it has never felt like merely a job. I love that it's also what I am paid to do – to raise the identity of teachers from employees to high performing educators, and to know that it will result in a compassionate school environment where children, like yours, will thrive.

But why is it so? What drove me to do this? What's my backstory?

So many events have had an impact on how I learn and teach, how I see others learn and teach, and why I help build authentic schools. And my backstory is a long one. I still have my very first school case, and in it are all my report cards, most of which describe me as bright and inquisitive, but far too talkative and sometimes disruptive. I can visualise exactly where I sat – in different classrooms and with very different teachers – for every school year from P-12, with one exception.

For a while, I believed this block – having no memory of Grade 2 – must be my backstory. But it didn't feel right. So I looked further back and 'saw' myself at five years old. Books, paper, pencils, school, and my dad's storytelling … I just couldn't get enough. My five-year-old self had already chosen a vocation. My backstory grew from a positive experience – an insatiable love of learning and teaching, which I still have.

Like me, there are thousands of teachers who thrive on being the best they can, and continue to strive for excellence in their chosen profession. Teaching is extremely rewarding; it is also complex and demanding. It could be said that those of us in the profession are learners, more than we are teachers.

To be a teacher

The word teacher can be traced back to the Greek term *deiknumi*, which means 'to point out' or 'to show'. Great philosophers, including Adler, Socrates, Confucius and, more recently, Rudolf Steiner, were educators of the highest order. Their work was to understand and 'to point out' what it is to be human, and how to live a peaceful and fulfilling life. They concerned themselves with issues of ethics, spirituality, wisdom, faith, politics and tradition. And, as we saw in previous chapters, as civilisation progressed, there was also a shift in education: learning with a trusted, private tutor-philosopher gradually evolved into the teaching of students *en masse* in formal places of learning – schools.

What exactly was to be taught in these places, and who would be qualified to teach there, also went through an evolutionary process. The consequence: the introduction of formal qualifications, and of teaching as a profession.

The makings of the teaching profession

In New York, during the late 1800s, industrialisation and technology generated enormous wealth for some, but also created deep economic divisions and a great deal of uncertainty as to how the future might be viewed. At about the same time, in a kitchen garden in Greenwich Village, NY, a school was established, to teach cooking, sewing, hygiene and other life skills to poor immigrant women. If these practicalities were to be taught in a relevant and meaningful way, it was obvious that the first step – and an essential one – was to have a deeper understanding of these women's backgrounds. A new pedagogy had begun, and soon more and more women began to teach the poor.

With the help of philanthropists, including the Rockefeller and Macy families, and the donation of a parcel of land from the Vanderbilts, the kitchen garden evolved into a school dedicated to teacher education. It would be called Teacher's College. Scholars, practitioners, philanthropists and thought leaders began linking theories, research and practice to improve teacher education, which involved tackling the issues of health, education, crime and cultural diversity of the time.

The Teacher's College became known for exploring the interrelationship of education, psychology, and health. This process, combined with the works of many great philosophers, including those mentioned earlier, has shaped the way in which teaching qualifications are acquired and, more importantly, how schools function today.

Teach for Australia

Like many other nations, Australia established Teachers Colleges where students learned how to teach. The early 2-year certificate courses involved studies in child development, sociology, psychology and philosophy, and included specific content knowledge in mathematics, English, music and science. During the 1980s, most Teachers Colleges were closed, and teaching qualifications were obtained from Universities – as they are today – after a four-year course of study.

The transition from Colleges to Universities and from a two-year course to four-year degree has resulted in changes to course content, and a greater breadth of subjects on offer. The changes haven't necessarily resulted in higher quality across the profession; they have, however, increased the diversity of thought, views and values.

Pedagogy – the art and science of teaching

My personal library is home to my childhood literary treasures. The 1953 *Victorian Reader* sits next to a collection of Enid Blyton books, including my absolute all-time favourite *The Adventures of Pip*. These personal classics hold the secret to my evolution – from student to teacher, teacher to educationist, and educationist to advocate of the teaching profession. They are the classics that taught me how to become a teacher.

On my very first day as a full-time teacher, I was faced with a harsh reality: I had learned very little at University about what to teach in reading and writing. I knew less than I needed to about child development in this area, and even less about the depths of pedagogy. That reality check was the catalyst for me to look back at my love of books when I was a child, and to view my students as I viewed myself at their age. And so began my passion for learning to teach, and teaching to learn – particularly in the area of English Language and Literacy.

During my workshops, I often share this story with teachers, and it astounds me that they generally feel the same way: that they were not as well prepared to teach a range of subjects as they would have wished to be. Great teachers like these are never afraid to acknowledge shortfalls, and to take action to remedy them.

Teachers are just like you. They have strengths, limitations, talents, values and attitudes that influence their life view and their professional conduct. While we like to think that teachers have control over what they teach, it is not the same as saying that what is taught is always under control. Take another look at the visual representation of pedagogy in Figure 6. Notice again the hidden curriculum, as well as the professional and personal qualities that influence pedagogy.

We cannot ignore the reality that families also influence pedagogy, to some extent. Comments made at the dinner table, your political persuasions, and even the snacks included in your child's lunch box, all influence the way your children view and discuss the world. Your opinions and views can be expressed indirectly – through your child – to influence the views and the lives of others.

Roles and responsibilities

It's not uncommon for parents to place a high level of trust in teachers. It makes sense to assume that, as professionals whose purpose it is to work with children, all teachers possess immense knowledge, wisdom and integrity.

However, the teaching profession is no different from any other. Every school has its share of outstanding teachers, who take their job seriously and provide a service above and beyond expectations. And, as in any other profession, there are also those with lesser degrees of capability or commitment.

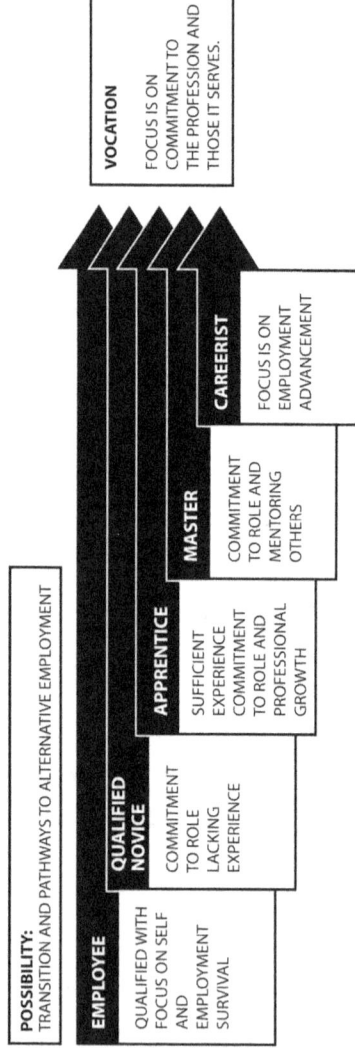

Figure 8: The Commitment Continuum
to what degree is a teacher devoted to self and others

If you went to a hairdresser you would expect to be satisfied with the service; otherwise, you wouldn't go back. Similarly, you would feel it necessary to have a trusting relationship with your medical practitioner, and make accurate disclosures, so that effective assessment, treatment and ongoing care could take place. The same can be said for the teaching profession.

During their careers, teachers move along what I call the **commitment continuum** (see Figure 8). Most teachers will be at different points on this continuum at various times in the course of their working lives. Here are some questions to consider asking your child's teacher:

Years of service

- How long have you been teaching?
- Which year levels have you taught and for how long?
- At which other schools have you taught?

Expertise

- What was your subject major during pre-service training?
- Do you have any other degrees or qualifications?

- What do you most enjoy teaching?
- In which area of teaching do you feel the least confident?

Extra responsibilities

- Beyond teaching, what other school responsibilities do you have?
- Do they take you away from the classroom? If so, who teaches my child at that time?
- Do you have the support you need to manage your workload?
- Are there other duties essential to your role, or can they be delegated to others?

Your advocacy for your child will open pathways towards a mutually trusting relationship.

The better you understand your child's teachers the better position you will be in to support them in teaching your child well.

Summary

In this chapter we've established these points:

- Teachers Colleges were places for students to learn the art and science of teaching
- Teachers Colleges have been replaced by Universities
- Curriculum content knowledge is one aspect of being an effective teacher
- Teaching is a complex profession
- Teachers have strengths and limitations
- A trusting relationship between parent and teacher is important

Taking the Lead

Use these action starters for taking the lead in your child's education:

- Talk to a number of teachers about their roles and responsibilities beyond teaching.
- Share your findings with other parents.
- If it appears that distractions are negatively affecting teachers, take your findings to the School Council or School Board.

Becoming Literate - The Home-School Connection

Chapter 5
BECOMING LITERATE - THE HOME-SCHOOL CONNECTION

*Children won't comprehend words
like sludgy, gooey and squishy
from an electronic device,
but from getting their hands dirty.*

John Wooden, the great UCLA basketball coach, is known for two things: winning seven consecutive NCAA championships between 1967 and 1973, and being one of the greatest inspirational leaders, basketball has ever produced. The first lesson he taught his players was to tie their shoelaces. His reasoning was: "This is a game played on your feet. If you get blisters, you can't play the game". For him, it was about getting the groundwork right, and laying the foundation for his players to develop all the skill sets they needed to become champion basketballers. The same can be said for becoming literate.

Becoming literate

At the end of WWII, the United Nations Educational, Scientific and Cultural Organisation (UNESCO) was established to promote peace and goodwill across the globe, and to prevent another world war. The founding nations of UNESCO believed that education would provide the means to achieve world peace. The result was a UN agreement that every child had the right to basic education and literacy.

As a result, the global-humanitarian march toward basic education and literacy began. It also sparked what has since been a costly, and seemingly endless debate about what it means to be literate. The debate involves questions such as: 'What defines literacy?' 'What is the acceptable minimum standard of literacy?' and 'What are the benchmarks of capability that determine what should be taught in schools?'

According to most dictionaries, to be 'literate' means to be able to read and write, to be educated, or to be knowledgeable in a particular area. According to UNESCO, 'A literate person is one who can, with understanding, both read and write a short simple statement on his or her everyday life' (UNESCO 1958).

But to what extent? Would being able to recognise and write your name suffice? Would marking an X on a piece of paper qualify as a signature, and therefore denote literacy? Is 'good enough', good enough? Or should we expect more – such as the ability to use words well? Should we look to the great philosophers and scholars of the past, to the work of Plato or Shakespeare, or to a time when rhetoric – the art of effective or persuasive speaking or writing – was taught and admired?

These are difficult questions. How do we know we are literate? What is good enough for your child?

Lessons from the thrift store

My partner and I recently attended a conference in the USA, and during our trip we enjoyed exploring unusual bookstores and thrift shops. I came upon a fabulous teaching guide, published in New York in 1886. The book begins with the basic learning symbols – the English alphabet – and ends with proofreading marks, which are the symbols used to edit manuscripts. In between are 100 practical and sequential lessons for the teaching of elementary (Primary) English grammar – lessons on prepositions, conjugations, particles, interjections, adverbs and clauses, to name a few.

Remember, this book was published in 1886 – almost 60 years before the United Nations was established. The standards expected in elementary schools at that time were more rigorous than those standards of primary school teaching in the late 60s and early

70s, when I went to school. I was not taught English Grammar at that depth when I trained as a generalist primary teacher during the 1980s.

It left me asking whether UNESCO's phrase, *'basic education and literacy'* had been taken too literally. I wondered whether governments around the world, in the quest to educate children on such a massive scale, had 'dumbed down' the meaning of education and literacy. And, in the process, had education just become big business? Governments, corporations, foundations, not-for-profits, volunteer organisations and publishers all have interests and involvement in schools, and in contributing to a literate world. But who is taking the lead? This question needs a great deal more discussion.

For now, consider this phrase: *'To understand and to be understood'*. I use it in my workshops to link rhetoric and grammar with what is taught and what is expected to be learned in the teaching of English. We can use this phrase to examine the intended curriculum, and explore what 'becoming literate' currently means for your child (see Figure 9).

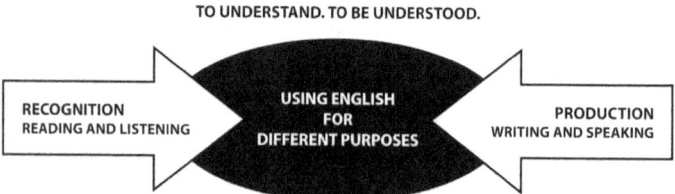

Figure 9: Becoming Literate:
Curiosity–Independence–Application–Mastery

Laying the foundations

To become literate, children need to recognise and produce symbols – the 26 letters of the English alphabet. They must be able to manipulate them, to construct words and combine them with others to create meaning. Words they can recognise and produce form a bank or collection, to which they continually add new words – especially those they encounter in the subjects offered in the curriculum.

We all have our own unique bank of words – more commonly known as vocabulary. We access or recognise vocabulary whenever we read and listen. We produce and use our bank of words whenever we speak and write (see Figure 9).

This doesn't mean, however, that your children always use their bank of words accurately. To become a competent user of symbols, or the alphabet, your child must study the conventional way in which words are produced, or spelled, in order to apply them to reading and writing. This is called orthography, the conventional spelling system of a language – in this case, English.

There are three layers of orthography and they are used interchangeably to teach children how to recognise and produce words. The first layer is *letter-sound*, the second layer is *pattern* and the third layer is *meaning* (see Figure 10).

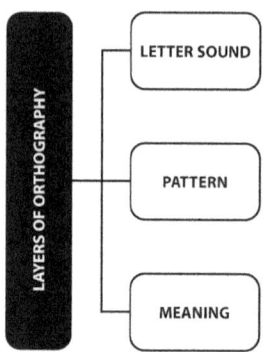

Figure 10: The conventional spelling system

Letter-sound

You probably know letter-sound by its alternative name – *phonics*. It refers to the relationship between the symbol or letter and the sounds it can make. There are 26 letters in the English alphabet, but they can make more than 40 sounds and, depending on the way letters are combined, they don't always make the same sound when they appear in a word. Phonics is one teaching approach, and one strategy your child might use. But to rely on letters and sounds alone is to limit the size of our word bank or vocabulary.

Pattern

Recognising and producing words requires knowledge of how letters can form patterns. For example, in the words *pear*, *pair* and *pare*, children cannot rely on knowing how individual letters are related to sounds.

Instead they must recognise three patterns – three combinations of letters producing words that sound the same. Understanding the many, often irregular, letter patterns in the English language, means children become more skillful, and more sophisticated, in reading and writing.

Meaning

The third layer is meaning. Understanding the meaning and origin of words, and parts of words, is the final stage. In the previous examples – *pear, pair and pare* – it is necessary to know the meaning of each word, as well as the different letter patterns, if we are to understand the word (in reading) or use it accurately (in writing).

The third layer also involves studying the Greek and Latin origins of words, and understanding the influence these languages have had on English. For instance, a basic or root word like *read* is adapted – by adding the prefix *'pre'*, meaning 'before' – and changed into *pre-read*.

Unless children learn how to recognise and construct words, they can't apply more complex grammatical rules or rhetoric to what they try to understand (by reading) or communicate to others (by writing).

Comprehension

'To understand and be understood' is another way of saying 'to comprehend and communicate'. This is being literate – the key to success in all other subject areas.

What has made the teaching of the English language so difficult is not the act of teaching, but the prior understanding of what is to be taught. Graduate teachers walk into schools today, as I did years ago, with enthusiasm and the ability to teach; they are not necessarily fully aware of what to teach.

Perhaps schools should take something from basketball coach John Wooden's approach, and get the groundwork right. Then there might be fewer debates about literacy and more emphasis on teaching the essential foundational skills.

Children's literacy affects everything they do. What is 'good enough' for *your* child? If you are to 'take the lead' in your child's education, it's important that you understand what literacy means, and what it looks like in the curriculum and the classroom teaching at your child's school.

The value of play

When my brother and I were young we would make mud pies. We'd sit in our grandparent's veggie patch, digging the dirt, adding water and throwing our concoctions against our grandfather's green garage wall. We knew very well what *squishy*, *muddy*, *dirty*, *sloppy* and *grainy* meant. We certainly didn't Google the words; we just got our hands dirty. We interacted, we lived in the moment, and we learned in the moment.

Playing like this, climbing trees, going on picnics with our parents, listening to bedtime stories, and cooking with Nan... all these experiences gave us a wonderfully rich childhood. They helped build our vocabulary and expand our understanding of the world around us, and we used what we learned, through playing and living, to learn even more. In school, your children will be encouraged to draw on their life experiences, too. Accessing 'prior knowledge' or 'making connections' is as important a part of becoming literate as a working knowledge of the language itself. The two combine to make meaning – a requirement for being literate.

The play and the life experiences you provide for your children, or share with them, are powerful. Through them, you contribute to the building of vocabulary and meaning that will help strengthen their ability to access and apply the English language right across the curriculum.

Home reading

Since the establishment of Education Acts during the late 1800s, Australia's colonial school curriculum relied on books – referred to as readers – and monthly school newspapers to establish and supplement skills in reading and writing; the focus was on English literature, history, and non-denominational moral values. The teaching of English became the responsibility of schools.

In 1917, mothers started to become involved in school life. First they were invited to observe their children in the classroom, and later they would visit the school each month to read stories to the children. This initiative was so successful that Mothers Clubs were founded, creating opportunities for further involvement.

During the late 70s and early 80s, New Zealand researcher and teacher, Don Holdaway, pursued his interest in the connection between home, school and reading. His studies focused on the relationship between mother and child during the bedtime story. He found the safe, nurturing, and compassionate environment to be naturally conducive to learning, and he believed that if the same atmosphere could be created in classrooms, then children's literacy rates would improve.

You might be familiar with the oversized books used in junior school classrooms. These are used in shared reading, which mimics the mother-child bedtime story experience. Just like the bedtime story, everyone can enjoy the story without the need to identify every word on the page. The teacher does most of the reading, while the children observe and join in where they can. Some classrooms replace the large books with interactive white boards that display the text.

Beyond the bedtime story, home reading has also become a common feature of the home-school connection. During my workshops, this topic is often raised as an area of concern. While home reading is not mandated by any legislation, most schools believe it to be an essential step toward your child becoming literate. Many schools believe your role is paramount in your child's success in reading and writing.

Although it's important that you provide your child with life experiences and prior knowledge, and your help and encouragement in home reading are invaluable, you should never feel that you are expected to teach reading strategies.

Teachers are qualified to teach English – including the teaching of reading. Your role is to nurture your child's love of reading, and enjoy the bedtime story and the relationship it builds between you and your child. Through reading you can encourage inquisitiveness and a desire to learn. If the home reading involvement your child's school expects from you is making a positive contribution, then that's great. If not, then don't participate.

Literacy, technology and the 21st century

My grandfather – or Gramps as we loved to call him – lived to the age of 97. He went to his grave feeling that he had failed, that he wasn't literate, and that he hadn't kept up with change. But Gramps' achievements were not measured by tertiary qualifications or preparation for life in the 20th century.

He dropped out of school in the second grade, to bring in an income to help the family. He lived through a number of wars, the Great Depression, the introduction of television, the first landing on the moon, and the invention of the mobile phone. He raised four beautiful children, and was known as Gramps to 14 grandchildren and 31 great-grandchildren. Gramps' name appears in an historical publication of Carlton and United Breweries. He was a non-drinker, but he was one of the first men in Australia to drive a truck, rather than a horse and cart, to deliver beer. He served during World War II, repairing aircraft in Papua New Guinea, and later he was chief gardener for his local council – a role that required him to drive a tractor.

In 2002, just before his passing, UNESCO delivered a new statement on literacy: 'Literacy is crucial to the acquisition, by every child, youth and adult, of essential life skills that enable them to address the challenges they can face in life, and represents an essential step in basic education, which is an indispensable means for effective participation in the societies and economies of the twenty-first century.'

My Gramps lived a full and rich life. He embraced technology and change. By any definition, he was a literate man. His life epitomised the 2002 UNESCO vision.

As your child's school career continues, technology will evolve, and schools will be challenged, and seduced, by computer coding, new reforms and research opportunities. We should keep in mind, though, that innovation and change have been rolling through human history since the time of the hunters and gatherers. We must make sure that the seductive call of technology does not tempt us away from other necessary skill sets. Their loss would be too great an expense to the community.

And neither should we forget that the best way to help our children acquire a love of the English language, and build vocabulary, is through conversation. Face to face, eye to eye interaction is the most powerful method of all. Replace television with conversation, smart phones with books, and encourage pen and paper rather than computers. Talk to your children often and leave the formalities of becoming literate to the professionals.

Summary

So far we've covered these points:

- Becoming literate includes the ability to read and write
- There is no finite point at which one arrives at literacy
- Knowing what to teach is critical
- Conventional spelling is known as orthography
- There are three layers of orthography – letter sound, pattern and meaning
- To comprehend is to understand
- Schools teach English in different ways
- Schools involve parents in the teaching of English, also in different ways

Taking the Lead

Use these action starters for taking the lead in your child's education:

- Ask your child's teacher to explain how English is taught.
- Turn off technology more often.
- Don't underestimate the power of play.
- Review the school policy on home reading.
- Campaign for parent information evenings, so parents have a better understanding of how English is taught.

Assessment and Reporting

Chapter 6
ASSESSMENT AND REPORTING

1 + 3 = 4 and 2 + 2 = 4.
Both are equal, yet they are not the same.

My standing promise to my two daughters is that, whenever possible, we visit their countries of birth – Thailand and Hong Kong – either for a holiday or a stop-over to another destination. We make sure each trip is filled with all kinds of new experiences, but eating out and trying different dishes is the talking point of every visit. Given we spend so much time in the kitchen together, it's no surprise that we all have an interest in food.

When my girls were older, we added cooking classes to our itineraries. The most recent one was during a trip to Thailand. It was an exceptionally good experience as it included a tour of the local markets. We had a fabulous time – sampling the fresh produce, learning more about how to select familiar, and uncommon ingredients and, of course, creating our own five-course meal.

All three of us absolutely love Thai green chicken curry – to the point that we tease each other about being connoisseurs of this particular dish. As it happened, this dish featured in our cooking class, so not only did we have to prepare and present our curries, but critique one another's as well. Needless to say, the teasing stopped and the competition began.

What impressed me most during this cook-off wasn't the outcome – which, not surprisingly, was that my Thai-Australian daughter won – but rather the teaching. Our host made sure that every intricate detail of preparation was just right – especially the curry paste. She demonstrated, observed, reinforced and acknowledged our efforts. We weren't shown any particular step until the previous one had been completed to her high standard. In effect, it had become *our* standard, because she brought out our desire to do well, our pride in our efforts, and our respect for the process. More importantly, she taught us how to taste as we cooked, to make sure the ingredients were well balanced and to our liking. When we walked away from our cooking experience, we were not only delighted after having had such a great day, but we felt we had heightened our claims to be connoisseurs. We now know how to define a great curry and describe exactly how we might modify the ingredients to improve a mediocre one. We're still enjoying becoming masters of the great Thai green curry. It was a day of teaching, learning and assessment at its finest.

What is assessment?

Having come this far in the book, I'd be surprised if you haven't formed an opinion or shared your point of view on something I have written. In some instances, you might have considered the importance of my stories, the quality of information provided, or perhaps the value of the visual representations.

Whenever you do these things, you make a judgement or assessment of the content and, I dare say, of me, the writer. This is what happens in classrooms every day. Teachers make judgements about your child's behaviours and actions – whether in terms of acquiring, practising, mastering, applying or reframing the intended curriculum. And they make final conclusions about their learning too. Assessment is a constant and necessary component of teaching and learning.

Types of assessments

Assessment comes in many forms and occurs at different times. You might be familiar with the terms *formative* and *summative* assessments.

Formative assessment is, in essence, what I described when I shared my cooking story. As we cooked we made judgements, and adapted texture, ingredients or flavours as we went. Formative assessments are done to modify the teaching and learning along the way to achieving the desired outcome. Examples of this in the classroom are questioning, student self-reviews, observations, quizzes, discussions and graphic organisers (written records of thinking).

Summative assessment, on the other hand, is what happens at the end of the journey. We make evaluations or judgements, and compare outcomes against particular benchmarks. In the cooking class, it was the look, texture and taste of each of our curries, and how it compared with the others. In schools, summative assessment might take the form of weekly spelling tests, national assessments and end-of-year exams.

Assessment and teacher judgement

During the 80s and 90s, Canadian school provinces began a review of their curriculum and testing schedules. They found that some provinces regarded summative assessments very highly and followed strict testing schedules. In other provinces, where there was a greater balance between formative and summative assessment, schools took a more constructivist approach to learning, with greater emphasis on including children in the formative assessment of their own learning.

In practice, both types of assessments have tremendous value. Both types also take into consideration *quality* – for instance, the content or perspectives in an essay – and *quantity* – for instance, accurate spelling and grammar or the number of correct answers in a test. Despite the type of assessment, or its timing, it is essential in the first instance to have a full understanding of what is being assessed.

Teacher judgement and your child

Let's revisit your assessment of this book and of me. As you read, you are making judgements, asking questions, internalising, and perhaps already taking the lead. Your assessment might affect your behaviour, but it won't change the content of this book.

If you were to comment, ask questions, or share your actions with me now – which I hope you will – it might lead to another book, a series of webinars for parents, a new blog or a weekly newsletter. Your judgements are not measured against those of others, and what happens as a result is entirely up to me.

However, if you were my editor, things would be different. By using the services of an editor during the writing process, I had every opportunity to improve the quality and content of this book. Her assessments involved feedback and recommendations, and her skillful crafting of the English language has taught me more about good sentence structure and effective word choice. The process therefore involved redrafting, more than once, of particular sections of the book – aspects that you cannot see in the final product.

If I had published my first draft, without the input of my editor, and what she taught me, this book would have appeared with errors of spelling, grammar, and punctuation and even of fact. It could have been a complete disaster.

How, then, could we assess or measure the success of this book? Would it be through your feedback or actions, and the flow-on to other work I might produce as a result? Would we perhaps consider my own learning, after working with my editor? Could success be measured by the number of books sold? Would you agree that 'all of the above' might apply?

You should ask the same of your child's learning and your child's teacher. If children could learn on their own and become 'masters' on their own, there would be no need for schools. That isn't how it works. Powerful learning evolves only from powerful teaching. And powerful teaching requires a thorough understanding of what must be taught and what this looks like when it has been learned. It demands a working knowledge – moment by moment and day to day – of what a student needs. More importantly, it requires a desire to act and to take action.

Powerful learning requires the capacity to listen, observe and understand informed teacher judgements. It demands discipline and a clear understanding of a task's purpose. And it too requires action.

Good teachers assess their own teaching as well as their students' learning. Great teachers seek counsel, to improve their teaching, and maximise student learning. Extraordinary teachers act on what they have learned and teach students to do the same (see Figure 11).

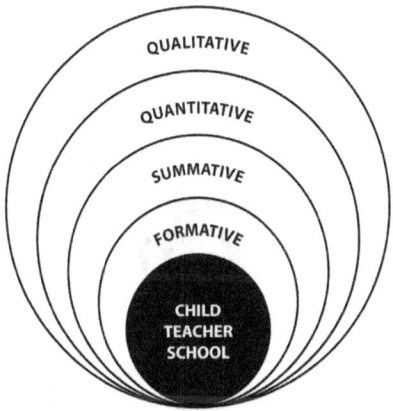

Figure 11: Assessment beyond the student

Reporting educational outcomes

Australia has developed the *Melbourne Declaration on Educational Goals for Young Australians* (2008), which is a nationally agreed education agenda for Australia for 2008-2018. The document outlines an agreement between the States and Territories, made to ensure

Australian schools provide the best educational outcomes for all children. The agreement states: 'Schools play a vital role in promoting the intellectual, physical, social, emotional, moral, spiritual and aesthetic development and wellbeing of young Australians, and in ensuring the nation's ongoing economic prosperity and social cohesion.' Figure 12 provides a visual representation of what the governments of the day consider to be absolutely necessary for schools to be involved, in the life of your child.

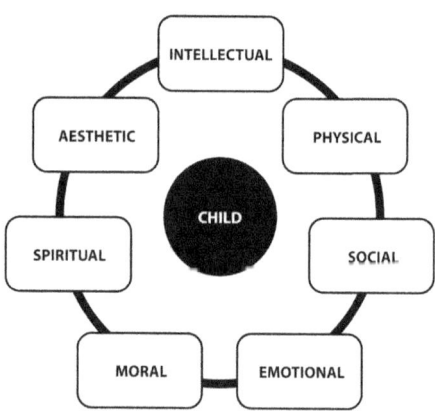

Figure 12: 2008-2018 School's Vital Role in the Life of Your Child

Achieving 'best educational outcomes' includes the school's responsibility to report effectively on your child's performance and progress. Look at Figure 12, and answer these questions: What does your school currently report on? To what degree should schools involve themselves in these areas? Are these areas evident in your school's policies and in its strategic plan for curriculum and reporting?

Reporting on teaching and learning

It is generally accepted that schools offer two parent-teacher meetings per year. The first is primarily designed as an informal introductory meeting. The second is usually held at about the mid-year mark, to coincide with mid-year reports. It is usually at this second meeting that your child's progress to date will be discussed.

This effectively means that, unless there is a glaringly obvious reason for you to request an additional meeting, you will not receive any report on your child's progress until halfway through the school year. This brings us back to the *Melbourne Declaration on Educational Goals for Young Australians* (2008).

When you enrol or re-enrol your child, request a meeting with your child's teacher at the same time: don't wait for the introductory meeting. Find out how the Melbourne Declaration has had, and will have, an impact on the intended curriculum and on your child's day to day, face to face learning experience. For example, ask your child's teacher what vital role the school is playing in your child's emotional, spiritual and moral development? This is an essential question for all schools, and even more important if your child attends a public school.

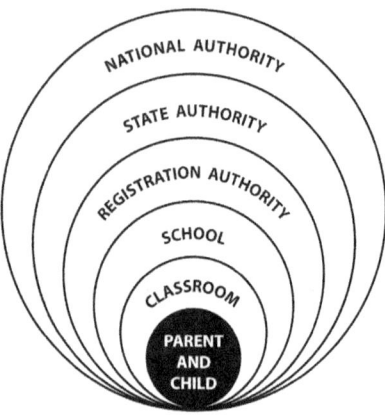

Figure 13: Layers of Influence on You and Your Child

Australia began as a Judeo-Christian society. Its first laws, and the subsequent Constitutions for each of its States were based on values that came from those traditions. When public schools were first established, they were also guided by these same values. So the question is this: If schools are expected to deliver a 'secular' education, then what are the spiritual and moral views being promoted? What does this look like in the classroom and how are those views measured or assessed? How does this situation affect you and your child?

Remember too, that your child is one of many in the class. If other children hold different spiritual and moral values, what might be the impact on your child? As an advocate for your child, you might also need to be an advocate for other children and families, and potentially for your child's teacher. The goal is to find out how government and school policies play out in the classroom (see Figure 13).

Reporting on assessments

At this introductory meeting you should also find out how the teacher makes judgements about your child's learning. Be sure to ask for an explanation of assessments, and find out how they are linked to the curriculum.

Mid-year report

As discussed in an earlier chapter, a mid-year meeting generally lasts for approximately 10 minutes. This is insufficient time for thorough reporting. Here are some suggestions about how to 'take the lead' and have a more effective mid-year interview.

1. Don't have an interview before you have received your child's report card.
2. If the teacher intends to refer to samples of your child's work, request a copy before the interview so that you are already familiar with their content.
3. Review the samples against the school curriculum.

4. Mark the sections you would like to discuss and make a list of questions.
5. Provide a copy of your questions so that your child's teacher also has time to prepare for the interview.

Reporting to families

A number of years ago, I joined the fundraising and the policy development committees of my daughter's local public school. I was looking forward to the involvement for two reasons. First, it meant that I could make an active contribution to the school and its reporting back to the community. Second, I would better understand the impact of these committees on teaching and learning, as it affected my daughter. In fact, I learned more about the school culture than I did about the committees.

The fundraising committee

At the first meeting we were informed that during the year the parent community would have to raise $110,000.00 to meet the costs of necessary school purchases. We were handed a list of items such as: books, electronic equipment, sports equipment, furniture for the staff room, plants, a BBQ, additional shelving, and so on. I asked whether the list of items was compiled in order of priority; the answer was no. I asked whether this could be done; the response was "Why?" I went on to ask, in the event we couldn't raise all the money, what must be purchased first, and what would come off the list. Furthermore, I wanted to know what would be the impact on teaching if those items were, or weren't, purchased. After much discussion, the school staff on the committee acknowledged that the budget and requests had come from School Council and were therefore out of the committee's control. Our main purpose was to meet the school's teaching and learning needs more effectively. Therefore we requested further elaboration from the Council, so as to have a clearer list of priorities in mind, before we began our fundraising.

Policy development committee

The first and only meeting I attended took place at the home of a parent, who had been involved with the school for a number of years. I was new to the school. The item on the agenda was the writing of a 'Visitor's Policy'. I watched as teachers and parents struggled and disagreed over wording, references to departmental policies, and concerns about privacy. After an hour and a half, I asked whether anyone on the committee was a lawyer, to which the answer was no. Why then, I wondered, were we spending so much time on the wording of a school policy that might prove inadequate anyway? Two of the four parents chose to continue writing. The other parent and I chose to campaign for a lawyer to join the committee. The result we intended was that the committee would not be involved in writing subsequent policies, but would focus instead on maintaining the schedules for policy updates and notifying staff and parents of changes.

School performance and culture

Australia currently has a number of tools that provide information about school performance. They offer a 'snapshot' at the national and State level, and enable comparisons between schools. Spending time comparing schools, however, won't necessarily produce better outcomes for your child. Instead, your energies would be better expended on becoming more familiar with your child's school.

Every school has a culture. The question is: what type of culture is it? Not an easy question to answer. Every school setting is unique, and when human interaction is the primary measure of a school's culture, to be fully aware of what happens in schools, and how to contribute, are considerable challenges.

If you want to start, at least, to learn more about the reports that come from your child's school, here are some suggestions:

1. Learn about the members of the School Council, their responsibilities, and the processes involved for meetings and elections.
2. Find out the composition of the Council – how are staff, parents and community represented?
3. Read the weekly newsletter.
4. Ask your child's teacher to help you review the annual school report and the strategic plan.
5. Request the agenda items and minutes of School Council meetings, if they are not already provided.
6. Attend the occasional school assembly or School Council meeting.

Assessment and reporting are often seen as things that are 'done' to students. Just as no amount of reporting on students will shape a respectful school culture, it's also true that no amount of student assessment will improve teaching; teaching, too, should be assessed.

Summary

In this chapter, we've covered these points:

- In schools, assessment is about making an informed judgement about behaviours and actions that affect teaching and learning.
- Formative assessment takes place over time to help 'form' future decisions about teaching and learning.
- Summative assessment is a concluding judgement at the completion of a teaching and learning cycle.
- Qualitative assessment is a judgement that cannot always be measured accurately.
- Quantitative assessment is a measurable judgement.
- When and how schools report to their communities is a reflection of their culture.

Taking the Lead

Use these action starters for taking the lead in your child's education:

- Learn the types of assessments your school uses.
- Become familiar with school policies on assessment and reporting.
- Familiarise yourself with the school's strategic plan and annual report.
- Get to know what your child's teacher needs, and advocate where necessary.
- Go beyond the school to learn all you can about policies and agreements at State and national levels.

Work-School-Family-Life Impact

Chapter 7
WORK-SCHOOL-FAMILY-LIFE IMPACT

*Time measures your actions,
not their impact.*

At the age of 3, my youngest daughter began her transition from a physically active climbing enthusiast, to a disciplined and highly skilled elite gymnast. Her interest in the sport came as no surprise: when I met her at 9 months of age she was already able to walk. Being invited to join an international squad at age 5 was exciting, but not without its challenges. Family life changed overnight. Chauffeuring her between gymnasium, school and home took precedence over other duties, and there were changes in income, a new budget, the ceasing of holidays, and much less time together as a family. The greatest challenge, however, was balancing school expectations.

By Year 4, my daughter's training commitments increased to 26 hours per week. She still went to school, and although full-time attendance wasn't possible because of the gruelling schedule, she was still expected to be accountable to a full-time workload. By the time she reached Year 7, her first year of secondary school, training had increased to 30 hours per week, and her workload at school had more than doubled.

You might argue that school is more important than gymnastics. Believe me, many times I wondered whether I was doing the right thing by my daughter in allowing the situation to continue. Her gymnastics training, however, was developing discipline, motivation, self-esteem, grit, teamwork, and a profound regard for her peers that no amount of schooling could provide.

Putting those things aside, we faced a reality. Schooling was compulsory and school expectations had to be addressed. As a teacher, I understood, although I didn't always agree with, the school's perspective.

There were numerous emails, phone calls and meetings. The school, on the one hand, was determined that my daughter should complete every assigned task, and I, on the other, was determined that she complete what was essential, and be exempted from what was not.

The coordinator was most understanding; some teachers, however, weren't, and my daughter's work continued to pile up. Anything that wasn't completed at school was either added to her homework load, or she was expected to attend homework club during lunchtime, which left little time to spend with her peers. Alternatively, she would be given extensions to complete her work later. When I asked what would happen at the end of the year when there was no more 'later', it was agreed that the situation required a more thorough review.

I created a colour-coded timetable of my daughter's standard week. Between wake-up time of 5.30am and bedtime at 9.30pm, the visual chart clearly shows how my daughter's time was spent (see Figure 14). The staff were now better able to appreciate what my daughter was trying to manage. Her training time of 30 hours per week was almost one third more than a teacher's classroom teaching load. Her travelling time in the car was almost 8 times more than a teacher's lunch break. Her time at school included lunch breaks, which meant her actual class attendance – and therefore face-to-face teaching and learning time – was well below that of her peers. An agreement was finally made: where possible, duplication of tasks and assessments would be reduced. It was an appropriate and balanced win-win for all concerned.

Balancing school with life

The term 'work-life balance' has been around for decades. Some major corporations have managed to

116 THE ULTIMATE PARENT TEACHER INTERVIEW PARENT GUIDE

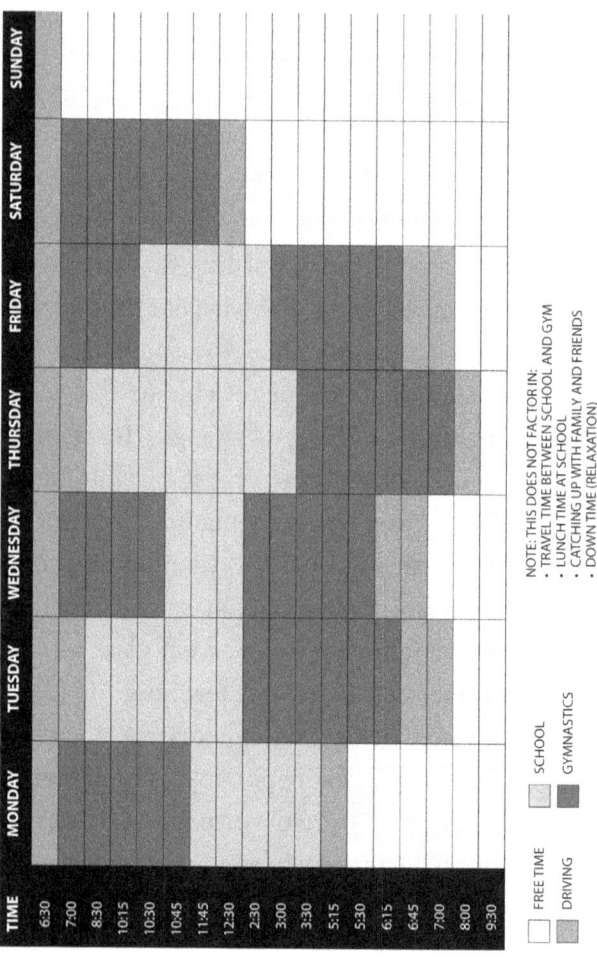

Figure 14: School-Life-Family Balance

provide a range of initiatives, but successful models have generally been limited to head-office premises. Families without access to that type of infrastructure must be more creative and, just as importantly, must negotiate flexible arrangements independently – unless they are connected to advocacy groups such as unions. Genuine regard and assistance for a work-school-family-life balance simply don't exist. You won't have that balance unless you advocate for it.

Let's take a look at the harsh reality of the imbalance in work-school-family-life.

Your child will attend classes for approximately 5 hours per day, or 25 hours per week. Your child's teacher's will attend to those classes for less than that – approximately 22 hours per week. So, even before your child begins a school day, there is an imbalance between face-to-face learning and teaching.

When additional workloads are added to this, the imbalance can be extraordinary. For your child, there are school-related demands – expected homework, home reading, among others –that impinge on family, social and personal time, including yours. Your child's teachers most likely have other duties beyond teaching that might be of concern.

A 2016 survey conducted by the Victorian Branch of the Australian Education Union (AEU) pointed to these statistics:

1. Teachers are overworked: 80% of teachers

work 15 hours of unpaid overtime every week.

2. Teachers are working an average 53 hours per week.

There are five key reasons why I raise this issue.

1. The out-of-school-hours work expected of your child can affect your entire family. If you are balancing a job, profession, or career, and the care of other children, the complexities are even greater.

2. If the work-life situation for teachers is as extreme as that indicated by the AEU, then it will most likely affect their capacity to deliver essential teaching; your child will be part of the fallout.

3. If your child's teacher is also a parent, there is the additional implication of managing work-school-family-life, which will have a further impact on teaching, and therefore on your child.

4. If you are a teacher, and you fall into the 80% category, how does your own work-school-family-life balance affect your teaching, your child's school life, and the children in your class?

5. In 2016, the Australian Bureau of Statistics

showed that in Australian schools there were more than 3.5 million full time students, and almost ½ million teachers, of which 70% were women. Communities right across the nation are affected, even if they are not directly connected to a school.

You might like to ask yourself these questions:

- What is your child's school contributing to your work-school-family-life imbalance, and for what purpose?
- Is there genuine value in such an overwhelming workload being placed on children, teachers and families?
- Why are schools making such demands on family and community lifestyles?
- Does your school employ the remaining 20% of teachers who can enjoy a more balanced work-school-family-life model?
- What does this model look like?

The eight hour day

During the 1850s, Victorian tradesmen worked 16-hours a day, six days a week, in the harsh Australian climate. It took its toll on their health and left little time for them to become better skilled and educated. More importantly, it detracted from their efforts to be better husbands, fathers and citizens. Life was tough and it was out of balance. The lives of employers, employees and indeed all Victorian families were affected. The solution was the eight-hour working day, leaving eight hours for leisure and eight hours for rest. This was a triumphant outcome that changed the Australian way of life. However, as we have seen, it didn't last and it would appear that schools played a central role in the return of the imbalance.

Homework

In the majority of schools there is the expectation that students do homework. While there is no legislation requiring it, schools and parents believe in its value. Their beliefs, however, do not necessarily match.

In my workshops, teachers often ask about ways to manage the demands parents place on schools to set homework. My answer always includes the word 'purpose'.

Homework is set for students. It does not, or should not, require any input from anyone else. The teaching that takes place in school should end there. If your child does not understand any homework given, then you should not be expected to step in on behalf of your child's teacher.

So what is the 'purpose' of homework? There are just three reasons why homework should be set – and even those are questionable.

1. To complete work
2. To prepare for a future task
3. To revise

Look at Figure 15. I've put these three reasons into two categories – Purposeful and Pointless Homework.

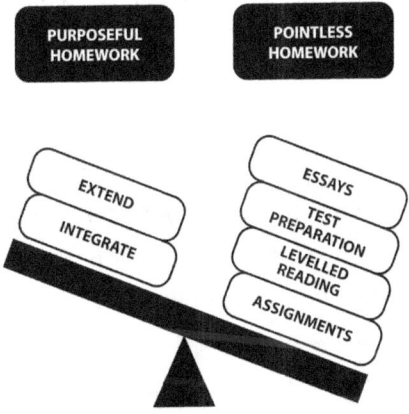

Figure 15: Value of Homework

Purposeful homework

Purposeful homework extends a child's capacity to master or apply new knowledge or skills. There is no need for teaching and no need for correction. These experiences are about your child's self-directed manner and drive to improve and apply previous learning. In this instance homework should in no way be compulsory; neither should it require your input – other than your encouragement and reflection.

Pointless homework

Pointless homework is that which will be marked or assessed, or which requires qualified intervention, such as the reading of levelled texts. This is teaching. Any task requiring teacher input should not take place at home.

Disclosure

Jeremy and Susan came to their child's first parent teacher interview of the school year. Their daughter, Sarah, was in my class and their son was two year levels above. They talked briefly about Sarah's strengths and limitations, and about their busy lives. They also informed me that they were separated but had shared custody, so Sarah moved between two houses. Their expectation was that any and all communication regarding Sarah would be provided to each of them. I respected their commitment and didn't need to know any more than they had shared. The information exchanged was sufficient for me to fulfill my two obligations: to be the best possible teacher I could for Sarah and to report her learning to both parents. Nothing more, nothing less. Beyond that, their private life was none of my business.

Teachers are service providers. Just like doctors, childcare workers and all other service providers, they are paid to provide their expertise so as to support you in raising your child. Keeping their focus on your child's progress, while maintaining your privacy, are their essential responsibilities. The teacher must handle whatever affects your child's learning, regardless of the details of the issue. In the example above, my position was to be aware of any changes in Sarah's behaviour, differentiate my teaching accordingly, and notify both her parents if necessary. It was not for me to know anything else, unless there were a custody or access restriction, which would be essential information. The details were not my business. Your personal matters are certainly not the business of your child's teacher. Be mindful, too, that children have a way of sharing personal information, and as with all professions, some education professionals have a way of asking questions. Maintaining your privacy might also require you to discuss boundaries for your child, and their teachers.

Let's flip this incident over for a moment. If your child's teacher were separated or divorced, in normal circumstances your interest would be in the teaching alone. This is the way to maintain appropriate responsibilities and mutual understanding.

Finance, demographics and privacy

Schools are communities, made up of individuals and families – including teachers and other members of staff – with diverse backgrounds. Most decisions a school makes are respectful of its community; sometimes, however, they are made with limited or no appreciation of the impact they will have on families.

Whether you are in the process of selecting a school, or your child is already in school, the points outlined in Figure 16 are worth considering.

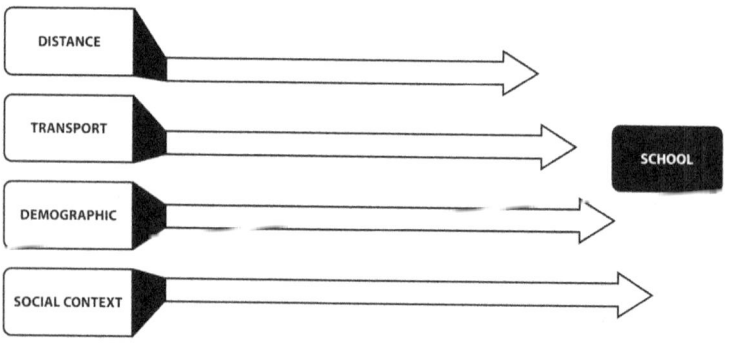

Figure 16: Economic Influence on School

Distance

What's the distance between your home or work and your child's school? Schools usually hold out-of-school-hours events throughout the year. Consider the impact of additional travel, childcare costs for other children, working time, family time, and budget.

Transport

Will you need to drive to school or use public transport? Consider the implications for your time, fuel costs, car maintenance, time management, and work, as well as the impact on other family members.

Demographic

Every school has its own demographic, which does not always match school location. For instance, independent schools found in exclusive suburbs might educate children from middle and low income families – due to scholarships and other charitable income sources. Likewise, children of parents born overseas are not always English language learners, so a high migrant area does not necessarily equate to poor performance or disadvantage. Becoming a part of a school community includes becoming a part of a wider demographic. Consider the values that are similar to, or might differ from, those of your family.

Social context

School offers a social context as well as a learning environment. A school's location and its demographic can influence expectations at social events – including children's birthday parties, parent functions and fundraising events. There is also the associated cost of your child, 'fitting in' – for example, in terms of fashion and footwear, camps and excursions. Consider the impact of these on your family, but when making choices for your child, consider also the situation other families face.

Summary

In this chapter we have covered these points:

- School expectations can affect work-family-life balance.
- Work-family-life commitments can have an impact on schools.
- You are your child's greatest advocate in balancing work-school-family-life issues.
- Teachers do not have a full-time teaching workload.
- Additional roles and responsibilities outside of teaching can affect your child.
- Teachers are service providers, with specific responsibilities.
- Disclose only what is necessary and place boundaries around personal information.
- The work-school-family-life issues of other school community members can affect yours

Taking the Lead

Use these action starters for taking the lead in your child's education:

- Create a timetable and block out times that you are content with the school's impact on your work-family-life balance.
- Review the school policy on homework and discuss it with your child's teacher.
- Start conversations with other parents to understand their views on homework and school influence.
- Attend a School Council or School Board meeting. If you need to field possible recommendations, you should know who represents your children.

Taking the Lead

Chapter 8
TAKING THE LEAD

Don't ever allow yourself to be treated as anything less than a respected advocate for your child.

Cathy had four young children. Two were in primary school, and two were enrolled in the childcare centre and kindergarten that I owned and operated. She was raising her children on her own, and in quite difficult circumstances. My staff and I willingly supported her with regard to everything that came under our duty of care and service. It became evident, however, that Cathy's needs were greater, and more complex, than we thought – and beyond the scope of any advice we were qualified to offer. Instead, I set in motion a plan to seek support from a number of other service providers, who would help her in parenting her children. Our service certainly owed a duty of care to Cathy's children, but this did not imply any right to assume the role of a parent. We were there to help Cathy with that role.

On a personal level, however, I chose to help Cathy. I offered assistance in preparing her CV, did some role-play for job interviews, and even gave her some of my clothing – including suits and shirts. Within months, Cathy had secured a full-time job. It was a position she thrived in, and her family life began to turn around.

Like childcare services, schools have similar responsibilities, and must also set similar boundaries. Learning to navigate them isn't always easy – for schools and for you, as parents. If you are to take the lead in advocating for your child, it's important to start by becoming aware of the balance that must exist – between home and your child's education at school.

The family in the life of a child

In September 1990, the *United Nations Convention on the Rights of the Child* – a statement about the care and assistance of children – came into force. Comprising 54 articles, its overarching preamble states: 'the family as the fundamental group of society and the natural environment for the growth and well-being of all its members and particularly children, should be afforded the necessary protection and assistance so that it can fully assume its responsibilities within the community.'

In other words, the statement acknowledges your right and responsibility to raise your children. However, it is also understood that services are available to assist you to do so. Schools fall into this category and their assistance is limited to the services they can provide.

It is fair to say that if teachers and parents do not have a thorough working knowledge of these services, in their day to day interactions with one another, the balance of care and responsibility can sometimes tip. Parents can be overly trusting, teachers can be overly enthusiastic, and both can be overly cautious.

Advice to parents

While scanning laws, regulations and curriculum in preparation for writing this book, I found a paper[2] that highlighted the issue of giving advice in pre-schools in Iceland. This nation, like many others, encourages cooperation between homes and pre-schools. It provides parents with information on their child's development and situation at pre-school. The paper's author pointed out, however, that there is no legislation stating that giving advice to parents is part of a pre-school teacher's job description or duties. The same applies to teachers and schools in other parts of the world, including Australia.

---
2. *The National Curriculum Guide for Pre-schools: Iceland*, 1999:35

This raises a number of questions:

1. What should be included in pre-teacher training to maintain essential boundaries between providing qualified information and offering opinions, with regard to your child's education?

2. To what degree should schools expect parents to be responsible for matters that fall within the responsibilities of a qualified teacher – for example, home reading?

3. To what extent can schools influence parents' trust in terms of what is seen as appropriate content in the intended curriculum – for example, sexuality education, or anti-bullying programs?

4. To what extent should parents expect schools to provide advice on parenting, education, or other matters?

5. What is the appropriate balance between home and school education?

The term 'whole child' is often used in describing a school's accountability, which includes the provision of healthy, safe, engaging, supportive and challenging education (see Figure 17). What does this accountability look like in your child's school? To what degree might the home-school boundaries be blurred? Talk to your child's teacher about the school's stand on educating the 'whole child'.

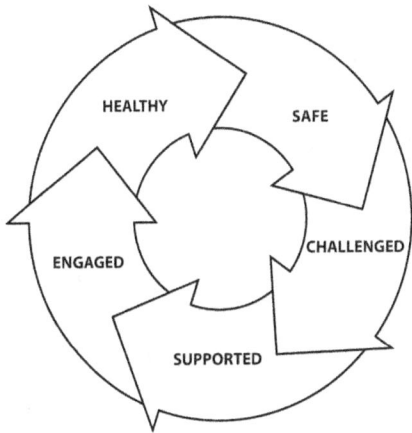

Figure 17: Educating the Whole Child

Schools and service to the community

Throughout the book there are numerous examples that illustrate the evolution of schools and the teaching profession. While we can examine both, predominantly as providers of education, it is worth reflecting, too, on the matter of 'service' beyond education.

In 1930, at the beginning of the Great Depression, the State Schools Relief Committee – a voluntary organisation – was established in Victoria. Controlled by teachers, its purpose was to distribute food and clothing to families in need. Thousands of parents and children right across the state benefitted from this support. However, according to the report from the Department of Education Victoria in 1933, children, too, were among those who donated to less fortunate children and their families. Citizenship, it would seem, was at its finest in Victorian schools during the Great Depression.

Apart from this relief, schools created stronger connections between home and community by arranging a series of clubs. Families and children could participate in the rearing of stock, the cultivation of flowers and vegetables, and the study of birds and insects. Various other clubs were involved in forestry, gardening, bands and orchestras, mobile libraries, sports, and a Junior Safety Council. Clubs provided support for parents in raising their children, while providing a healthy connection between home and school.

There were also partnerships between schools and businesses, including the State Bank, where children were encouraged to open bank accounts and learn the value of saving. Almost 45,000 children were members of the Junior Red Cross; cash and in-kind services provided support for those in need and, for the students, membership was great for 'character building' and encouraging good citizenship.

The State Schools Relief Organisation exists to this day, and still donates school uniforms and footwear to children in need. The clubs established during the Depression influenced the expansion of the intended curriculum. They have either been adapted to suit current day practice – for example, school bands – or other organisations, clubs or tutors provide similar services. Schools continue to evolve and will do so well beyond our lifetime.

While no-one would deny that the relationship between home and school is a powerful one, what can be debated is the degree of power it has. If they complete Year 12, your children will be at school for just 13 years of their lives. This isn't a huge portion of a whole lifetime, but for a child it is more or less the whole of the life they have known.

Balance and reason

What would you do if the school took your child away from you? It sounds like an outrageous question, doesn't it? Nevertheless, it's one I would like you to take seriously. Every day decisions are made in schools and classrooms. You might agree with most of them; some, however, can 'remove' you from your child's life. To balance the influence of home and school there must be a genuine reason for any and all decisions made.

In 1964, a report on the future of tertiary education in Australia, stressed that, 'education enables the individual to make choices and decisions at personal and political levels which are well-informed and objectively assessed.'[3]

---

3. *Report of the Committee on the Future of Tertiary Education in Australia to the Australian Universities Commission.* Volume 1, August 1964

At the school level, this includes you. Matters of interest or concern, whether at a general or a personal level, affect you, your child, your family and the wider community. Your child's teacher, the School Council or board, school committees, and the school generally should, therefore, have two important goals: to keep you well informed, and to encourage your objective contribution.

From my personal and professional experience, I believe four fundamental principles are involved in well-informed and objective participation: Capacity, Reliability, Integrity, and Compassion.

Capacity: Makes clear distinctions between qualification, opinion and authority

Reliability: Establishes healthy boundaries between trust, disclosure and opinion

Integrity: Demonstrates the ability to rise above influence and opinion of others

Compassion: Involves moving beyond empathy and towards action, in a given situation

Figure 18: Conscious and Balanced Decision-making

If you apply these principles, in every interaction you have with your child's teacher and with your child's school, you will be on the way to forming a genuine parent-teacher relationship. The support that home and school provide one another will strengthen your child's education.

Use your voice to build genuine relationships between home and school, and between parent and teacher. Be confident in supporting others to do the same.

Some suggestions:

1. Don't just accept decisions. Think critically.
2. Go beyond 'wants'. Advocate for what your child 'needs'.
3. Turn talk into action. Build a support network.

Only two questions remain: What action do you need to take? When will you take it?

Take the lead. Raise your child. And above all else, enjoy a balanced and genuine home-school relationship. And start now.

Checklists
TAKING THE LEAD

THE SCHOOL

- [ ] I have met the school principal.

- [ ] I am aware of application procedures.

- [ ] I am aware of the registered authority to which the school is accountable.

- [ ] I am familiar with the school zoning policy.

- [ ] I have an understanding of the school's faith, life view or philosophy.

- [ ] I have been informed of the teachers who will have direct responsibility for teaching my child.

- [ ] I know where to access key school documents – including strategic and annual plans, policies and reports.

- [ ] I have met the office staff.

NOTES

SCHOOL COUNCIL - SCHOOL BOARD

☐ I am aware of who represents the school at Board/Committee level, and their responsibilities.

☐ I know where to obtain information regarding School Council or board agendas, meetings, reports and election processes.

NOTES

CURRICULUM

- [ ] I am familiar with the curriculum at my child's current year level.

- [ ] Someone has explained to me the purpose of assessment and other procedures related to the curriculum.

- [ ] I understand the responsibilities my child's teacher has, and I feel confident about requesting additional services where necessary.

- [ ] I know where to find additional information about the school curriculum.

- [ ] The school's reporting procedures are clear.

- [ ] I understand how to read my child's report card.

- [ ] I am comfortable with speaking to my child's teacher about matters relating to the curriculum.

- [ ] I am comfortable with being an advocate for my child, and I understand the procedures involved.

NOTES

A Final Note

A FINAL NOTE

'When human beings meet together seeking the spirit with unity of purpose then they will also find their way to each other....'
– Rudolf Steiner

I hope you have enjoyed this book. It takes courage to take the lead, and I am thrilled that principals, teachers and parents have encouraged me in my efforts to make a stand for authentic and productive relationships between parents and teachers.

I have tried to present the content in an accessible and easy-to-read form. That's my way of reaching out and encouraging you to 'take the lead' as well.

Please write to me at **cheryl@cheryllacey.com** to ask any questions you might have, or to share your goals and achievements. Only by working together can we help others build genuine parent-teacher relationships in our schools.

You can visit my website at **www.cheryllacey.com** for more ideas and resources.

INDEX

accountability 8, 134

Adler 63

alphabet 50, 77, 79-80

assessment xii, 69, 91, 93, 95-97, 107-109

balance xiii, 13, 96, 115, 117-118, 120, 127-128, 132-134, 137

community xi, xiii, xv, 7, 9, 19, 33-34, 36-39, 45-46, 87, 104, 107, 119, 124-125, 127, 132, 135-136, 138

Comprehension 82

compulsory 18-19, 27, 36-37, 114, 122

Confucius 18, 63

curricular xi, 47, 55

curriculum xi, 33, 37-39, 42-43, 45, 47-51, 53-58, 67, 71, 78-79, 82-83, 95-96, 101, 103, 133-134, 136

Ezra 33

face-to-face teaching 115

faith 17, 19, 32, 38, 40-42, 63

feedback 23, 97-98

funding 3, 38

history 41, 61, 84, 87

homework xii, 25, 115, 117, 120-122, 128

Judeo-Christian 102

literacy xii, 48, 66, 76-78, 82, 84, 86, 88

pedagogy xi, xii, 50, 54, 57, 64-67

philosophy 40, 42, 65

principal 5-6, 20, 51, 53

pupil-free 23

schedule 22, 114

School Board 20, 72, 128

secular 36-38, 102

services 18, 27, 46, 97, 132-133, 136-137

Steiner 63, 147

Teachers Colleges 65, 71

technology xii, 38, 64, 86-87, 89

tutor 18-19, 34, 55

vocabulary 79-80, 83, 87

www.ingramcontent.com/pod-product-compliance
Lightning Source LLC
Chambersburg PA
CBHW071928290426
44110CB00013B/1514